Joseph Hume Francis

History of the Bank of England

A Comprehensive Account of its Origin, Foundation, Rise, Progress, Times and

Traditions...

Joseph Hume Francis

History of the Bank of England
A Comprehensive Account of its Origin, Foundation, Rise, Progress, Times and Traditions...

ISBN/EAN: 9783337062804

Printed in Europe, USA, Canada, Australia, Japan

Cover: Foto ©ninafisch / pixelio.de

More available books at **www.hansebooks.com**

HISTORY

OF THE

BANK OF ENGLAND.

A Comprehensive Account of its Origin, Foundation, Rise, Progress,
Times and Traditions, Manner of Conducting Business,
its Officers and Offices, and a full History
of the Bank and its entire Work-
ing and Management.

BY

JOSEPH HUME FRANCIS.

*THE FIRST COMPLETE HISTORY OF THE WORLD'S GREATEST FINANCIAL
INSTITUTION EVER WRITTEN.*

CHICAGO, ILLINOIS:
EUCLID PUBLISHING COMPANY.
1888.

TO

HON. WM. L. TRENHOLM,

COMPTROLLER OF THE CURRENCY OF THE UNITED STATES,

THIS

HISTORY OF THE BANK OF ENGLAND

IS,

WITH HIS KIND PERMISSION,

MOST RESPECTFULLY DEDICATED

BY THE AUTHOR.

PREFACE.

CUSTOM, which is as arbitrary as fashion, renders it necessary that this volume should be prefaced by the author.

This history is presented with the hope that it may impart useful knowledge regarding the life of the greatest monetary establishment in the world — something meagerly and imperfectly understood.

The chief merit claimed for this work is that of its being an extensive collection of facts connected with the history of the Bank of England, and of its foundation, rise and working and general management. Other subjects germane to banking and the Bank of England are touched upon. Every known source of information has been consulted, and in collecting and arranging the facts for the first complete history of the Bank of England only matters of interest and value have been treated, although we have in hand and have had the benefit of material extending over many centuries.

A rich store of knowledge may be obtained from books, but there are two entirely opposite methods of giving knowledge. The first is that which enters into extensive detail, and repels and confuses the average reader with scientific phraseology, meaningless tables and figures, and verbose description. The second is that which seeks, by simplicity and conciseness, to make knowledge attractive, entertaining and instructive. The latter is the method adopted in this volume. The aim has been to explain and elucidate all matters of real interest connected with the bank and its history.

We wish in this connection to thank several officials and employees of the Bank of England for courtesies extended, and also for placing at our disposal all information desired.

THE AUTHOR.

CHICAGO, Ill., December 1, 1888.

CONTENTS.

CHAPTER I.

ORIGIN OF AND FIRST BANKERS IN THE WORLD.—Bank First Mentioned in the Bible—Money Changers in the Jewish Temple—Origin of the Word Bank—People who Invented Banking—First Bank in Europe—All the Early Banks in Europe—First Bank in London—How Bills of Exchange Originated—First Funding System—First Permanent National Debt—Bankers of Greece and Rome—High Rates of Interest—Origin of Modern Banking—Goldsmiths as Bankers in London—English Country Bankers—Primitive Financial Methods—Necessity for Money—Fundamental Nature of Money—What Ancients Used for Money—When Gold and Silver were First Coined—Invention of Money—Money Made of Iron, Wood, Shells, Salt, Brass and Tin Current—Origin of Various Coins.................................. 13-29

CHAPTER II.

DUTIES AND USES OF BANKS AND BANKERS.—What is a Banker?—First Bank of Deposit—Interest from Borrowers—A Bank in its Simplest Form—How Profits are Derived—How to Pay Interest on Deposits—Security Against Fraud—Safest Way of Loaning Deposits--Securities Prudent Bankers Avoid—The Power of Credit—Keeping Deposits on Hand—The Many Uses of Banks—William E. Gladstone on Credit—Banks of Issue and Banks of Deposit—Advantages of Combining a System of Lending Money with that of Receiving It—Origin of English Pounds, Shillings, Pence, Guineas and Sovereigns—Thompson Hankey, an Ex-Governor of the Bank of England, on Bankers—Banking Schemes and Projects Prior to the Foundation of the Bank of England—The Idea of Credit Banks... 30-48

CHAPTER III.

FOUNDATION AND EARLY HISTORY OF THE BANK OF ENGLAND.—Why the Bank was Established—Origin of the Bank—The Governor and Company of the Bank of England—History of William Paterson, its Founder—He dies Unhonored and Neglected—Prophets who Predicted Financial Ruin—"The Old Lady of Threadneedle Street"—Paterson and his Ill-Fated Darien Scheme—Present Condition of the Bank—The Policy of the Bank Assailed by the Public—How the Bank is Officered—The Bank Charter—How it Reads—Restrictions, Impositions and Demands—Buying Property from and Lending Money to the Crown—Suspending Payment of Notes—Assistance from the Government Averts a Failure—Capital Increased—Confidence Restored—Length of Original Charter.................................. 49-63

CHAPTER IV.

HISTORY OF RENEWALS, DEBTS AND PANICS.—Advancing Money to the Government—How the Bank Receives Pay from the Government—Persecution—The "Dead Weight"—Table of Renewals of Charter, with Capital, Debt and Conditions of Renewals—An Explanation by an Ex-Governor of the Bank—Amount of Loans to the Government—Present Capital of the Bank of England—A Panic Quieted by a Novel Method—Merchants Come to the Bank's Rescue—The Bank Attacked by Rioters—Solidity of the Bank of England..................................... 64-78

CHAPTER V.

PROGRESS OF BANKING.—The Desirability of a National Bank—Success Brings Competition—The Scheme for a "National Land Bank"—Country Banks Issue their Own Notes—War for Independence in America—Great Industrial and Commercial Development—Startling Increase in Banks—Unreliable Bankers, Worthless Paper, Unlimited Credit and Prodigal Bankers Precipitate a Big Crash—Violent Revulsion in London—300 out of 350 Banks Compelled to Stop Payments—The Bank Assailed by Jealous Competitors—Its Triumph—Given Exclusive Banking Privileges—Banks Prohibited from Doing Business Within Sixty-five Miles of London—Sir Henry Parnell on Banking..................... 79-87

CHAPTER VI.

SUSPENSION OF CASH PAYMENTS.—Important Epoch in the History of English Banking—Passage of the Restriction Act—The Government Advises with the Bank—Run on Country Banks—Bank of England Again in Trouble—Suspension of Cash Payments—Embarking on a New Course—The Bank Issues a Notice to the Public—Increase in Country Banks in 1797—Cause of Enormous Failures—Extending the Field for Circulation of Bank of England Paper—History of Depreciation of Currency—Paper Raised to Par by Accidental Circumstances.................................. 88-98

CHAPTER VII.

SPECULATIONS, SCHEMES, FAILURES AND LOSSES.—Bank of England Resumes Cash Payments—Vicissitudes of Banking—Speculative Rage—No Scheme Too Hazardous—Speculation of To-day not Without a Precedent—Worthless Paper Readily Negotiated—Discounts Easily Obtained—Schemes of Country Bankers—A Cyclone of Failures—Bank of England Makes a Serious Blunder—Distrust Fully Awake—A Tremendous Run—Cause of the Difficulties—An Instructive Table—Accumulation of Securities—What the Directors Should Have Done to Avoid Disaster—Loss of Three Millions of Bullion—The South Sea Bubble—A Delirium of Speculation—List of the Bubble Companies in 1721—Getting Rich Without Trouble—Philanthropist Thomas Guy.............. 99-110

CHAPTER VIII.

LOOSE BANKING METHODS PARALYZE BUSINESS.— Improving Country Banking — Suppressing £1 Notes—Repealing

Laws—Circulation of Notes for Less than £5 Forbidden—Speculative Schemes Again in Abundance—Rage for Establishing New Banks — Voluminous Issue of Notes—Raising the Rate of Interest—Shock to Industrial Undertakings— How the Bank of England Escaped Failure—Natural Obstacle to Formation of New Banks—The Railway Mania—Gigantic Frauds Perpetrated by Projectors of Imaginary Railroads—The Country Wild with Speculation—The Crash Wrecks Thousands—A Banker's Duty—The Penalty of Neglect 111-124

CHAPTER IX.

BANK OF ENGLAND HANDLED BY PARLIAMENT.—The Famous 1844 Bank Act—Sir Robert Peel Battling for Reform—Providing a Remedy for Instability—Financial Writers Interested—Peel's Speech on the Renewal of the Bank's Charter—Important Provisions of the New Law—Price Paid for Exclusive Privilege of Banking—Suspending the Bank Act in 1866—Fundamental Principle upon which English Currency Rests—The Law and the Bank—The Bank's Control of Its Capital................... 125-135

CHAPTER X.

RADICAL CHANGES IN THE MANAGEMENT OF THE BANK.—Privileges of Officers and Directors—Groundless Nature of a Charge Often Made—Plausible Objections to New Laws—Amount of Notes Issued—How to Determine an Excess of Currency— Notes in the Banking Department — Great Changes Wrought in the Management of the Bank—Restricting Banks for the Issuing of Notes—Convertibility of Bank of England Notes—Variations in the Rate of Discount—Temporary Suspension of the Act of 1844 to Avert a Panic—Effect of Modification of Usury Laws—Particulars as to Number and Class of Depositors—Development of the Methods of Economizing Money — Transitory Credits—Discount Variations—Credit and Capitalists—No Change Probable in the Methods of the Bank of England—Should Banks be Prohibited from Issuing Notes—True Way to Remove Danger—Modification of Banking Laws—Bank of England Notes Made Legal Tender............................. 136-154

CHAPTER XI.

FRAUDS, FORGERIES, THEFTS AND DEFALCATIONS.—The First Forged Note on the Bank of England and Execution of the Forger—How Discovered—Counterfeiting—Decision of the Lord Chief Justice—Defeating Counterfeiters—Great Theft of the Head Cashier of the Bank of England—A Loss of £320,000—Inventing a Safety Paper—Men Executed by Scores for Counterfeiting—Ingenious Schemes for Swindling—Sir Robert Peel Victimized—Another Thieving Official — Fauntleroy Secures £300,000 by Forgery—A Rascally Clerk Escapes to the United States and is Apprehended—Losses by Forgery—A Chief Clerk Swindles the Bank to the Amount of £800,000—His Novel Method that went Undetected for Five Years—Bidwell's Million Pound Swindle...155-167

HISTORY OF THE

CHAPTER XII.

MANAGEMENT OF THE NATIONAL DEBT.—Management of all Other Stocks Held by the Bank—How the Work is Performed by the Bank of England—Stock Offices—Dividend Pay Office—Cheque Office—Unclaimed Dividends—Stock Office Library—Number of Books in Library—A Perfect System—178,000 Distinct Accounts—Register Office—Post Warrant Office—The Routine Work of Above Named Offices Described—Names of the Governors of the Bank of England from 1694 to 1888 168-178

CHAPTER XIII.

INTERNAL WORKINGS OF THE BANK OF ENGLAND.—Private Drawing Office—Public Drawing Office—What is Considered a Remunerative Balance—Working Accounts—Number of Bills Issued—Business in the Bill Office—Branch Banks, and How Conducted—Drawing Accounts and Discount Accounts—Important Service Performed by Branch Banks—Number and Location —Rules and Regulations Under Which Accounts are Received in the Bank of England—Denomination of Bank of England Notes. 179-189

CHAPTER XIV.

BUSINESS OF THE BANKING DEPARTMENT.—How it is Conducted—Amounts Cheques may be Drawn for—Opening an Account with the Bank—Business the Bank Transacts for Customers —Bank Deposits—Profits of the Bank—How Derived—Expenses of the Bank—Weekly Bank Statement Given and Analyzed—Proportion of Assets to Liabilities............................... 190-196

CHAPTER XV.

DISCOUNTS, DIVIDENDS, LOANS AND RULES.—Duties of the Discount Office—Precaution Before Discounting—Powers of the Directors—Who Are Allowed Discount Accounts—Checking a Speculative Tendency—Inconsistency of Long Date Discounts—Opinion of an English Writer—Real and Fictitious Transactions—Rules to Observe—Who Controls the Rate of Discount?—False Notions Regarding the Power of the Bank of England—Rate of Discount from 1794 to Date—Dividends on Bank of England Stock from 1694 to 1888—The Price of Bank Stock and How Bought and Sold...................... 197-206

CHAPTER XVI.

ENGLISH AND AMERICAN CLEARING HOUSES.—How they Originated in London—Primitive Manner of Conducting Business —How Transacted To-day and Amount of Business Annually Done —A Clearing House for Country Bankers—American Clearing Houses—Detailed Statement of the Routine Business in the New York Clearing House—Scene in the Clearing House During Business Hours—Specimen Credit Ticket—How the Banks are Represented and Settlements are Made—The Settling Clerk and Delivery Clerk—Duties of the Proof Clerk—Specimen Sheet of Clearing House Proof—Penalty for Making Errors—Specimen Sheet of Settling Clerk's Statement........................ .207-216

Chapter XVII.

BANK OF ENGLAND AND AMERICAN BANK NOTES.—Description of a Bank of England Note—How Made—Peculiarity of Design—Number of Notes Paid out Daily and Number Cancelled—How Burned and Destroyed—The Accountant's Library—Why Notes are Not Reissued—The Bank's Printing Office—Durability of the Notes—Cutting Notes in Two Pieces Sent Through the Mails—Curiosities in the Bank Album—Barlow's Remarks on Bank of England Notes—Antiquity of Bank Notes—United States Currency—How it is Printed, Worn Out and Destroyed—Workings of the National Bank Redemption Agency......................217-219

Chapter XVIII.

ISSUE DEPARTMENT.—NO INTEREST ON DEPOSITS.—Preparing Bank Notes for Use—How Notes Get into Circulation—Exchanging Notes for Gold—Inland and Foreign Withdrawals—The Bullion Office—Bank of England Purchasing Gold—Gold Weighing Room—Mechanical Accuracy and Dispatch—No Interest Allowed on Deposits—An Ex-Governor Defends the Policy of the Bank—A Tradition....................................220-237

Chapter XIX.

PRESENT MANAGEMENT AND DESCRIPTION OF THE BANK OF ENGLAND.—How the Bank is Officered and Managed—Qualification and Election of Officers—Salaries—Tenure of Office—Court of Directors—Bank Committees—Explanation of their Duties—Division of the Clerical Force—Working in Harmony—The Secretary and his Duties—Total Number of Employees in the Bank—The Enormous Salary List—Conveniences and Societies for Clerks—Library, Reading and Dining Room—Insurance and Guarantee Society—Medical Attendance—How Clerks are Appointed—Names of the Various Departments—Description of the Bank—Its Exterior and Interior—Number of Acres the Bank Occupies—Statue in Bank, with Inscription Thereon—How the Bank is Guarded—Officers who Reside in the Bank—Eminent Services Rendered by the Bank..............................238-253

Chapter XX.

ENGLISH AND SCOTCH BANKS.—Scotch Banks Not Affected by the Bank of England—First Scotch Bank—Its Founder—Capital and Distribution of Shares—Origin of British Linen Bank—Passing Through Commercial Crises—Minimum Deposit Received—Allowing Interest on Deposits—Responsibility of Shareholders—Superior Banking System—Taking Advantage of an Old Law—A Scotch Cash Credit—General Solidity of Scotch Banks—Resposibility of Bank Partners—Law on Attaching a Debtor's Property—Scotch and Irish Banks in London.....................254-260

Chapter XXI.

A FINANCIAL PRESSURE.— Definition of a Pressure — Dates of Principal Pressures — Speculation the Main Cause — Gilbart on Pressures—The Duties of a Banker—Pressure of 1847—Report of the Lords' Committee—The Government Asks the Bank of England for Assistance — Correspondence Between the Bank and the Government. 261-270

Chapter XXII.

A COPY OF THE CORRESPONDENCE Between the Chancellor of the Exchequer and the Bank of England, Relative to the Renewal of the Charter of 1844..................................271–287

Chapter XXIII.

AMERICAN AND ENGLISH BANKERS ASSOCIATIONS—Constitution of the American Bankers Association—Who are Eligible to Membership—Its Objects—How Conducted—The English Institute of Bankers—Its Constitution—Facilities Afforded to Members—Detailed Account of the Manner of Conducting Business..288–301

CHAPTER I.

ORIGIN OF AND FIRST BANKERS IN THE WORLD.

Bank First Mentioned in the Bible—Money Changers in the Jewish Temple—Origin of the Word Bank—People who Invented Banking—First Bank in Europe—All the Early Banks in Europe—First Bank in London—How Bills of Exchange Originated—First Funding System—First Permanent National Debt—Bankers of Greece and Rome—High Rates of Interest—Origin of Modern Banking—Goldsmiths as Bankers in London—English Country Bankers—Primitive Financial Methods—Necessity for Money—Fundamental Nature of Money—What Ancients Used for Money—When Gold and Silver was First Coined—Invention of Money—Money Made of Iron, Wood, Shells, Salt, Brass and Tin Current—Origin of Various Coins.

THE denunciations in the Bible, in Exodus xxii, 25, shows that banking institutions were of very ancient date. The earliest modern bank was that of Venice in 1171, which was finally closed by the conquest of the French in 1797. Several of the early banks began at the following dates:

Venice 1171	Rotterdam ... 1635	Berlin 1765
Geneva 1345	Stockholm ... 1688	United States. 1780
Barcelona.... 1401	Bank of England 1694	St. Petersburg 1780
Genoa 1407		Ireland 1783
Amsterdam .. 1607	Scotland 1695	France 1800
Hamburg 1619	Copenhagen .. 1736	

The National Banking system of the United States was established by Acts of Congress Feb. 25, 1863, and June 3, 1864.

In times when nations were chiefly engaged in pastoral or agricultural pursuits, the trade of banking would hardly suggest itself to anybody as a profitable calling; and until, in the progress of a community toward civilization, the extent of its commercial dealings had become very considerable, none would be led to give their attention to the occupation of facilitating the money operations of the rest of the mercantile community. It is probable that the necessity for some such arrangement would be first experienced in consequence of the different weights and degrees of fineness of the coined money and bullion which would pass in the course of business between merchants of different nations. The principal occupation of the money-changers mentioned by St. Matthew, by whom the sacredness of the Jewish Temple was invaded, was doubtless that of purchasing the coins of one country, and paying for them in those of their own or of any other people, according to the wants and convenience of their customers. It is likewise probable that they exercised other functions proper to the character of bankers, by taking in and lending out money, for which they either allowed or charged interest (*Matthew* xxv. 27). Little, however, is known with certainty regarding the nature of the money dealings of the ancient Jews.

In the time of Demosthenes, banking operations were carried on to a great extent in Athens. They exchanged foreign moneys, received deposits at interest, and gave loans. The bankers were generally of low origin, such as freedmen and aliens; but they frequently rose to great wealth and eminence.

Gilbart in his "Treatise on Banking" says the term bank is derived from *banco*, the Italian word for bench, as the Lombard Jews in Italy kept *benches* in the market place, where they exchanged money and bills. When a banker failed, his bench was broken by the populace; and from this circumstance sprang the term bankrupt.

In the year 1171 the City of Venice was at war with both the eastern and western Empires. The finances were in a state of great disorder, and the Great Council ordered a forced loan of one per cent. from every citizen, upon payment of interest at five per cent. Commissioners were appointed to manage the payment of the interest to the bond holders and the transfers of the stock. The citizens received stock certificates in exchange for the sums they paid, bearing interest, which they might sell or transfer to any one else. The original loan was called the Monte Vecchio; afterwards two other similar loans were contracted which were called the Monte Nuovo and Monte Nuovissimo.

At this period the Germans were masters of a great part of Italy; and the German word Banck came to be used as well as its Italian equivalent Monte, and was Italianized into Banco, and the loans on public debts were called indifferently Monti or Banchi, and the word was finally reduced to Banke; thus we find an English writer, Benbrigge, in 1646, speaking of "The three Bankes of Venice."

Galiani, an Italian historian, says: "Lombard Jews invented the business of banking in Rome in the ninth century, and were called *Argentarii*. They received the money of their clients much after the manner of the banks of the nineteenth century, who could give their creditors cheques on their bankers, as is also the modern custom. They also invented bills of exchange, and to send a draft for money was called *permutare*. We find in the middle ages an increase in the business of the Roman banks. As commerce increased in the prosperity of the eleventh century, they established correspondents in various parts of Europe and drew bills upon them called Bills of Exchange."

The meaning of the word bank was the same in English when it was first introduced. The essential features of all these early banks was that a number of persons placed their money in them and received in exchange for it, credit or a promise to pay, which credit they might transfer to any one else. The Bank of England was formed in a similar manner of a company of persons who advanced a sum of money to the government and received in exchange for it an annuity. This was the foundation of the national debt of Great Britain, and to the present day the funds are legally called "Bank Annuities."

During the Middle Ages, when commerce was but little developed, there was little field for banking operations; but the business was first established in Europe by the Lombard Jews in Italy, A. D. 808, of whom some settled in Lombard Street, London, where many bankers still have their places of business. It seems to have been revived in Florence during the early part of the twelfth century. From the success that attended the commercial enterprises of the Florentines, that city became the centre of the money transactions of every commercial country of Europe, and her merchants and bankers accumulated great wealth. At one time Florence is said to have had 80 bankers; and we find that between 1430 and 1433, 76 bankers at Florence lent the state 4,865,000 gold florins.

As previously stated, the earliest public bank in modern Europe was that of Venice, founded in 1171. It originated in the financial difficulties of the State, which, in order to extricate itself, had recourse to a forced loan from the citizens, promising them interest at the rate of five per cent. The stock was made transferable, and a body of commissioners, called the *Camera degli Imprestiti*, or Chamber of Loans, was appointed to manage the transfer of stock and the payment of interest. This is believed to be the earliest instance on record of the funding system, and the first example in any country of a permanent national debt. This Chamber of Loans, as originally instituted for the purpose of managing the public debt, could scarcely be called a bank; and it does not appear to have carried on anything like a banking business for several centuries. Venice being the centre of an enormous commerce, foreign coins, usually in a very worn or clipped condition, were in circulation, to the great inconvenience of merchants; and hence the State had recourse to the expedient of authorizing the Chamber of Loans to receive coins of all sorts, and to pay for them in notes an amount corresponding to the real amount of bullion deposited. These notes promised to pay the bearer on demand a definite quantity of bullion of the proper fineness. The bank, however, does not seem to have discounted bills on its own account. Its only advantage was to save the wear and tear of the coinage, and to insure a uniform standard in mercantile transactions. Its notes always bore a premium as compared to the current money of the city; and it continued to exist until the fall of the republic in 1797.

Banking appears to have reached a high state of development among the ancients. The bankers of Greece and Rome exercised nearly the same functions as those of the present day, except that they do not appear to have issued notes. They received money on deposit, to be repaid on demands made by cheques or orders, or at some stipulated period, sometimes paying interest for it, and sometimes not. Their profits arose from their lending the balance at their disposal at higher rates of interest than they allowed the depositors. They were also extensively employed in valuing and exchanging foreign moneys for those of Athens, Corinth, Rome, &c., and in negotiating bills of exchange. In general they were highly esteemed and great confidence was placed in their integrity. The rate of interest charged by the bankers was sometimes very high, but that was not a consequence, as has been alleged, of their rapacity, but of the defective state of the law, which, as it gave every facility to debtors disposed to evade payment of their debts, obliged the bankers to guarantee themselves by charging a proportionally high rate of interest.

Banking reappeared in Italy upon the revival of civilization. The bank of Venice is reputed the first in date in the history of modern Europe; but it did not become a bank, as we understand the term, till long after its foundation. Historians inform us that the republic, being hard pressed for money, was obliged, upon four different occasions, in 1156, 1171, 1480, and 1510, to levy forced contributions upon the citizens, giving them in return perpetual annuities at certain rates per cent. The annuities due under the forced loan of 1156 were, however, finally extinguished in the 16th century; and the offices for the payment of the annuities due under the other two loans having been consolidated, eventually became the Bank of Venice. This might be effected as follows:—The interest on the loan to Government being paid punctually, every claim registered in the books of the office would be considered as a productive capital; and these claims, or the right of receiving the annuity accruing thereon, must soon have been transferred, by demise or cession, from one person to another. This practice would naturally suggest to holders of stock the simple and easy method of discharging their mutual debts by transfers on the office books, and as soon as they became sensible of the advantages to be derived from this method of accounting, bank-money was invented. It will, however, be seen that the establishment thus described was at first no more than the transfer office of a National Debt, transfers of which were accepted at par in discharge of private debts, and it is indeed said that the funded debt transferred sometimes commanded a slight premium above the current money of the republic. This establishment was ruined, after passing through many changes, by the invasion of the French in 1797. Thus the origin of modern banking may be authentically and directly traced to the money-dealers of Florence, who were in high repute as receivers on deposit and lenders of money in the 14th century; and banking was indeed practiced at Florence in the 13th if not in the 12th century. Mr. Macleod writes (*English Banking*, vol. i. 289)—

"The names of the Bardi, Acciajuoli, Peruzzi, Pitti, and Medici were famous throughout Europe. In 1345 the Bardi and the Peruzzi, the two greatest mercantile houses in Italy, failed. Edward III. owed the Bardi 900,000 gold florins, which his war with France prevented him paying; and the king of Sicily owed them 100,000 gold florins. The deposits of citizens and strangers with the Bardi were 550,000 gold florins. The Peruzzi were owed 600,000 gold florins by Edward III., and 100,000 by the king of Sicily, and the deposits they owed their customers were 350,000 gold florins. The fall of these two great pillars of credit involved that of multitudes of other smaller establishments; the community of Florence had never been thrown into such ruin and disorder before. And thereupon he breaks out against the folly of his fellow-citizens, entrusting their money to the care of others for the love of gain. The city, however, recovered from this terrible disaster, and we find that between 1430 and 1433 seventy-six bankers at Florence lent 4,865,000 gold florins. At one time Florence is said to have had eighty bankers, but not any public bank."

The business of banking was not introduced into England till the 17th century, when it began to be undertaken by goldsmiths in London, who appear to have borrowed it from Holland. It was attacked as innovations commonly are. From a pamphlet published in 1676, entitled *The Mystery of the New-Fashioned Goldsmiths or Bankers Discovered*, a passage may be reproduced that will be found interesting:—"Much about the same time—the time of the civil commotion—the goldsmiths (or new-fashioned bankers) began to receive the rents of gentlemen's estates remitted to town, and to allow them, and others who put cash into their hands, some interest for it if it remained but a single month in their hands, or even a lesser time. This was a great allurement for people to put money into their hands, which would bear interest till the day they wanted it; and they could also draw it out by one hundred pounds or fifty pounds, &c., at a time as they wanted it, with infinitely less trouble than if they had lent it out on either real or personal security. The consequence was that it quickly brought a great quantity of cash into their hands, so that the chief or greatest of them was now enabled to supply Cromwell with money in advance, on the revenues, as his occasion required, upon great advantages to themselves."

Sir Josiah Child also attacked "that innovated practice of bankers in London" in his *New Discourse of Trade*, though he subsequently became himself a banker; and his house, Messrs. Child & Co., of Temple Bar, and the house of Messrs. Hoare, in Fleet Street, still survive as the only private banks now in existence in London which were established previous to the Bank of England.

Money matters in England were also for some time regulated by the Royal Exchangers, but their calling fell into disuse until revived by Charles I. in 1627. The royal mint in the tower of London was used as a bank of deposit until Charles I., by a forced loan, in 1638, destroyed its credit. The Goldsmiths Company, of London, undertook private banking in 1645, but on the closing of the Exchequer, in 1672, their transactions terminated.

It thus appears that in every country where money was in use, there the trade of banking seemed to follow as a natural consequence. According to the commonest principles of the economy resulting from division of labor, wherever money came into general use, there banking became a common trade, in the same way as the trades of butchers and bakers, all found equally useful in their respective ways for the distribution of articles of consumption in the most easy and in the most economical manner. Banking was the channel into which money passed almost as an article of commerce,—the mode by which the money, not immediately required by one individual, found its way to be used by another : the banker thus appearing to act, and really acting, in the double capacity of borrower and lender ; but in neither case was he a creator, but a mere distributor of capital, any more than the butcher performed any other functions than that of distributing the articles in which they respectively dealt, and thus contributing to the general wealth of the community by the economy of time and money effected by this general system.

Prior to the establishment of the bank of England, banking in London was conducted first by the Jews, who were succeeded by the Lombards, who were in turn supplanted by the goldsmiths. The latter lent money at rates much below those charged by their predecessors, and they issued promissory notes payable on demand, or at a certain period after date. These bankers deposited their funds at the royal mint in the tower of London. This practice was discontinued when Charles I., being in want of money, seized the amount thus deposited, £200,000, by which means the bankers were utterly ruined. During the civil war the business of the goldsmiths largely increased, and during the commonwealth, as well as subsequently, various plans were devised by different individuals for the establishment of public banks. No action was, however, taken to mature and carry out these plans until the establishment of the bank of England. After the seizure of the funds by Charles I., it was the practice of the goldsmiths to deposit their surplus means in the Exchequer, which funds were drawn once a week, to meet such demands as might be made upon their owners. Charles II., in 1672, being in want of money, closed the Exchequer, and seized the funds belonging to the goldsmiths, amounting to £1,328,562, on which there accrued 25 years' interest, making thereby a sum total of £3,321,313. No consideration was given for any part of this large sum, except £664,263, for which government loan was issued, forming the basis of the present national debt of Great Britain. As may readily be imagined, the goldsmiths were ruined irretrievably by this infamous proceeding.

The earliest country bank established in England, of which there exists any record, was at Newcastle-on-Tyne, in 1755. This was a bank of issue. From that period the number of these institutions increased. In 1694 the Bank of England was established.

In the primitive ages of the world we have abundant evidence that there was no such a thing as money. When persons traded, they exchanged the products directly with one another. Thus we have in Iliad, vii. 468:—

> "From Lemnos' Isle a numerous fleet had come
> Freighted with wine.   *   *   *   *
> *   *   *   *   All the other Greeks
> Hastened to purchase some with brass, and some
> With gleaming iron : some with hides,
> Cattle, or slaves."

This exchange of products against products is termed barter, and the inconveniences of this mode of trading were palpable. What haggling and bargaining it would require to determine how much leather should be given for how much wine, how many oxen, or how many slaves? Some ingenious person would then discover that it would greatly facilitate traffic, if the things to be exchanged were referred to some common measure. But the state of barter still continued, as it is quite common at the present day when the precious metals are used as money, to exchange goods according to their value in money. Such a state of things in no way implied money, or currency, or circulating medium.

The necessity for money arises from a somewhat different cause. So long as the things exchanged were equal in value there would be no need for money. If it happened that the exchanges of products or services among persons were equal, there would be an end of the matter. But it would often happen that when one person required some product or service from his neighbor, that neighbor would not require an equal amount of product or service at the same time, or, perhaps, even none at all. If then a transaction took place with such an *unequal* result, there would remain a certain amount or difference of product due from the one to the other, and this would constitute a debt—that is to say, a right or property would be created in the person of the creditor to demand this balance of product at some future time, and at the same time a duty is created in the person of the debtor to pay the product, or perform the service, when required.

Now among all nations who exchange, this result must happen:—Persons want something from others when those other persons want nothing from them. And it is easy to imagine the inconveniences which would arise if persons never could get anything they wanted, unless the persons who could supply these things wanted something in return at the same time. In process of time all nations hit upon this plan:—they fixed upon some material substance which they agreed to make always exchangeable among themselves to represent the amount of debt. That is, that if an unequal exchange took place among persons with a balance due from one to the other, then an amount of this universally exchangeable merchandise was given to make up the balance, so that the person to whom the balance was due might get an equivalent from some other person.

Thus is seen the fundamental nature of money, as this universally exchangeable merchandise is called; its especial and particular purpose is to represent the debts that arise from unequal exchanges among men, and to enable persons to obtain the equivalent of the service they have done to one person from some one else.

An old phamphleteer in 1710 writes: "Trade found itself unsufferably straightened and perplexed for want of a general specie of a complete intrinsic worth as a medium to supply the defect of exchanging, and to make good the balance, where a nation, or a market, or a merchant demands of another a greater quantity of goods than either the buyer had goods to answer, or the seller had occasion to take back."

But when we consider the purposes for which money is intended, it is easily seen that no substance possesses so many advantages as metal. The use of money being to preserve the record of services being due to the owner of it for any future time, it is clear that it should not be liable to alter by time. A money of dried codfish would not be likely to keep very long, nor would it be very easy divisible. One of the first requisites of money is that it should be divisible into very small fragments, so that its owner should be able to get any amount of service at any time he pleases. Taking these requisites into consideration, it is manifest that there is no substance which combines these qualifications so well as metal. It is uniform in its texture, and it can be divided into any number of fragments, each of which shall be equal in value to another fragment of equal weight; and if required, these fragments can always be reunited, and form a whole again of the aggregate value of all its parts. All civilized nations, therefore, have agreed to adopt a metal as money, and of metals, gold, silver and copper have been chiefly used.

MONEY AND PRECIOUS METALS FIRST DISCOVERED AND USED.

Salt is current in Abyssinia.
Codfish is current in Iceland.
Cakes of tea are used in India.
Shells are used in India and Africa.
Pieces of silk pass as money in China.
Bronze was coined in China 1120 B. C.
Silver coin was used in Britain 25 B. C.
Gold was first coined in Rome 207 B. C.
Silver was a metal known to the ancients.
Tin was coined by Dionysius I. of Syracuse.
Leaden coin is current in the Burman Empire.
Platinum was coined in Russia A. D. 1828—1845.
Gold is a metal known from the remotest times.
Silver money was not used in Rome before 269 B. C.
Brass money is spoken of by Homer as existing 1184 B. C.

Brass was coined in Rome under Servius Tullius 573 B. C.

Paper money was in use in the 13th century at Milan, Italy.

Cattle were used for money in ancient Greece and Rome.

Nails of iron and copper were used in Greece as the National coin.

Wampum was used by the American Indians as a purchasing power.

Skins of wild animals were used by the ancient Romans for currency.

According to Heroditus the Lydians were the first to coin gold and silver.

Quantities of pasteboard were coined in Holland A. D. 1574, and passed current as money.

The largest collection of coins, 125,000 in number, is in the cabinet of antiquities, Vienna.

Money was made of wood and leather by Numa Pompilius, King of Rome, about 700 B. C.

Money was coined in the Temple of Juno *Monenta*, from whence the English word money was derived.

The inner bark of the mulberry tree was cut into round pieces, stamped and used as money in China in ancient days.

The Parian Chronicle ascribes the first coinage of copper and silver money to Pheidon, King of Argos in Ægina, 895 B. C.

The ancient English penny, penig, or pening, was the first silver coin struck in England, and the only one current among the early Saxons.

The coin known as the guinea took its denomination because the gold whereof the first was struck was brought from that part of Africa so called.

In Britain as late as the Norman conquest two kinds of money was in use, *living money* consisting of slaves and cattle, *dead money* consisting of metal.

About A. D. 1635, among the Colonists of Massachusetts the prevailing currency was wampum, corn and beans; musket balls passed for a farthing apiece.

A *mint* was established at Camulodumum (Colchester), England, by Cunobelin, one of the native kings, during the reign of Augustus, where money was coined of gold, silver and brass.

Coin (*cuna pecunia*) seems to come from the French *coign*, that is, angulus, "a corner;" whence it has been held that the most ancient sort of coin was square with corners, and not round as it now is.

Cash, in a commercial style signifying the ready money which a banker, or merchant, or other person has at his present disposal, and is so called from the French term *caisse*, that is, "chest or coffer," for the keeping of money.

The etymology of the word *scylling* would lead one to suppose it to have been a certain quantity of uncoined silver; for whether it is derived from *pcylan*, "to divide;" or *pecale*, "a scale," the idea presented by either word is the same; that is, so much silver cut off, as in China, and weighing so much.

Though a pound is one of the most common denominations for money, it never was a real coin, either in gold or silver, in any age or country. Such large and ponderous coins would have been in many respects inconvenient. But for many ages, both in Great Britain and in other countries, that number of small coins which was denominated a pound in computation, or a pound in sale, really contained a pound of silver, and they might have been and frequently were weighed, as well as numbered, to ascertain their value. If the number of coins that were denominated a pound in sale, did not actually make a pound in weight, an additional number of coins were thrown in to make up the weight.

CHAPTER II.

DUTIES AND USES OF BANKS AND BANKERS.

What is a Banker?—First Bank of Deposit—Interest from Borrowers—A Bank in its Simplest Form—How Profits are Derived—How to Pay Interest on Deposits—Security Against Fraud—Safest Way of Loaning Deposits--Securities Prudent Bankers Avoid—The Power of Credit--Keeping Deposits on Hand—The Many Uses of Banks—William E. Gladstone on Credit—Banks of Issue and Banks of Deposit—Advantages of Combining a System of Lending Money with that of Receiving It—Origin of English Pounds, Shillings, Pence, Guineas and Sovereigns—Thompson Hankey, an Ex-Governor of the Bank of England, on Bankers—Banking Schemes and Projects Prior to the Foundation of the Bank of England—The Idea of Credit Banks.

A BANKER is the custodian of the money of other persons. Such is his business viewed in its simplest aspect. A banker, if he hoarded the money deposited with him, would be simply a cash keeper to the public; his bank would be literally a bank of deposit. Even were the business of banks limited to the keeping of deposits, it would be of no small advantage to society; the depositors would be retired from the care of their money and in many cases from the trouble of handing it to those to whom they required to make payment. If the person to whom the depositor wishes to pay money intends also to deposit it, a transfer in the books of the banker, from the one to the other, made on the order or check of the depositor, would effect the payment. The money itself would lie undisturbed. The Bank of Amsterdam, which was founded in 1607, was a bank of deposit simply. But the business of receiving money has almost always been, and is now universally, in all portions of the civilized world, combined with that of lending it out. A banker does not hoard all the money deposited with him—he gives the greatest portion out to loan. The lending of money is as much a part of his business as the receiving of deposits. For the money he lends he receives interest from the borrowers; and in this interest he is paid for his trouble in taking charge of the deposits, and for his risk of bad debts. The services that a banker performs as the cash-keeper of his depositors are great. In the case of persons, not themselves in business, it is quite usual for a banker to make all their money payments, beyond their small daily expenditures, and to receive the money payable to them.

A bank, in its simplest form, is an institution where money may be deposited for safe keeping; but banks are now established to lend as well as to receive money; and the profits of a banker are commonly derived from the excess of the interest he receives from those indebted to him over the interest he allows, so far as he allows any, to those who have deposited money with him.

When money is received on deposit it is commonly repayable to the depositor alone, to whom a deposit note or receipt is given, but it may be also paid to any one to whom the depositor gives an order on the bank.

If a banker undertakes to pay interest on deposits, the rate generally varies according to the length of the notice the depositor agrees to give before withdrawing the money, the ability of the banker to deal with it being, of course, dependent upon the time he may rely upon keeping it. When money is received on a current or drawing account the customer of the banker draws it out, as he requires, by means of orders, to which the specific name cheques is given. Partly for convenience and partly by way of security against fraud, bankers are in the habit of giving their customers books of forms of cheques consecutively numbered.

In a primitive state of society, where the community consumes immediately, or presently, all the produce of its labor, there can be no such thing as capital. All the community may be in a happy and comfortable condition, but so long as this state of things continues, it never can be possessed of capital. When, however, the same community, or any part of it, desires and finds it possible to lay by a part of its produce, that is to consume less than it produces, such surplus becomes capital.

A banker often makes advances upon the deposit of government securities, railway debentures, bills of lading, mortgages, municipal bonds, and such like; but, except the government securities, the others are generally looked carefully into by prudent bankers. Loans are usually divided into *short loans* and *dead loans*, the former having a fixed time for their repayment, the latter no fixed time. Loans of the latter class are generally avoided. Advances upon deeds, except in agricultural districts, are always objectionable. If depositors have the power of demanding the amount of their deposits of any kind from the banker, while he usually makes his advances for a fixed or definite period, it is evident that he must always have on hand, uninvested, a considerable sum to meet such claims. The amount necessary for this purpose may generally be pretty nearly estimated. It depends upon a number of circumstances; as the state of the money market, the amount and nature of the deposits, the average amount of daily payments, and the like. If a banker is at liberty to issue bank-notes to a certain amount, it is evident that the profit derived therefrom is equal to the interest upon the difference between the average amount in circulation and the amount of specie required to be kept on hand to meet them, less the expense of their manufacture. If, however, a banker were obliged to keep dead stock or bullion equal to the amount of his notes in circulation, he could make no profit. But for a banker in good credit it is considered that a 4th or a 5th part of this sum is usually sufficient. Besides serving as places for the safe custody of money, and allowing interest on deposits, banks are of great use in a safe and rapid transference of money from one place to another.

Banking is trading in and with money—buying, selling, exchanging, receiving and paying money—not money's worth, not goods, but money in some shape or form—that medium which is used in all civilized societies for denoting a certain exchangeable value, and thus rendering as simple and as easy as possible the mutual exchange of all the commodities required for the use of mankind.

In considering the advantage and economy derived by society from a system of banking, it is of essential importance to bear in mind this very general definition, because it is by no means unfrequently supposed that bankers possess great powers of adding to the existing wealth of the country by augmenting its capital—powers which cannot properly be attributed to them.

William E. Gladstone once said in a parliamentary debate:—

"Though banks afford a valuable assistance in the collection and distribution of capital, it must not be supposed, as is often done, that they have any direct influence over its formation. That is the joint effort of industry and economy—the former in producing convenient and desirable articles, and the latter in saving and preserving them for future use. Credit is neither more nor less than the transfer of money or other valuable produce from one set of individuals called lenders, to another set called borrowers—a transfer which is greatly facilitated by the establishment of banks. And as there can be no reasonable doubt that those who borrow have, in the majority of instances, better means of employing capital with advantage than those by whom it is lent, its transference from the one to the other will, in so far as this presumption is realized, be publicly advantageous. But this is the entire extent of the beneficial influence of what is called credit; and when it happens, as is too often the case, to divert capital into the pockets of knaves and gamblers, it is disadvantageous. No doubt we frequently hear of great undertakings being carried on by means of credit; but such statements are entirely false and misleading. They will, indeed, be uniformly found, when analyzed, to mean only that the undertakings are carried on by means of borrowed capital. Credit is impotent to produce anything whatever. It is, in fact, a mere name for the trust reposed by a lender in a borrower. To call it capital is as much an abuse of language as it would be to call weight color, or color weight. It may transfer money or produce from A to B, or from C to D, but that is all that it either does or can do. When credit is said to be high, nothing is really meant save that those who have money or capital to lend have great confidence in the borrowers, and conversely when credit is said to be low."

Among the instruments of civilization which the ingenuity and industry of man have given to his species, not one has been so completely characterized by the elements of potency of affect and universality of application as money, says Lawson in his ancient History of Banking. The love of gold has been associated in the minds of unphilosophical moralists with an inordinate appetite for wealth, oblivious of the truism that in the absence of money, the comparative productions of nature, and of the labors of man, might be appreciated, but could not be harmoniously adjusted. In the days when gold was not, swains might barter a sheep for a cow, and consider it a good bargain, but when those days of simplicity developed into days of wisdom, a more thorough appreciation of things took place. A very small quantity of the finest metals, such as gold and silver, being, by reason of their scarcity, of greater value than other commodities, because by common consent the means whereby all things necessary for man might be obtained; and in all ages they have been distinguished as precious metals by all civilized nations, and people have exerted their utmost industry and ingenuity in procuring them. But as even gold and silver were subject to be adulterated by the admixture of baser metals, certain standards were agreed upon by which to ascertain their purity; and their value was computed by weight, the unit of quantity being some known natural substance, the variations in which were supposed to lie within very narrow limits.

To conform to this measurement the pennyweight was devised. Henry the Third caused a grain of wheat gathered from the middle of the ear to be the standard weight; and, thirty-two of these, well dried, were to make one pennyweight; twenty pennyweights one ounce, and twelve ounces one pound Troy; then it was thought advisable to divide the pennyweight into twenty-four equal parts, called grains.

Before, however, we proceed to develop the progress of banking in England, a word will not be amiss on English money. Previous to the Norman Conquest, the mode of reckoning by the Anglo-Saxons was by pounds or pence. It is recorded that William the Conqueror introduced into England the method of reckoning by pounds, shillings, and pence, or by pounds, ounces and pennyweights. The pound weight of silver was divided into twelve shillings, composed of twenty pennies each—corresponding to pounds, ounces and pennyweights—or twenty shillings, of twelve pennies each, but it was not till some time afterwards that it obtained the denomination of the "pound sterling."

Antiquaries and critics are greatly divided in their opinion as to the origin of the word *sterling*. One writer attributes it to the Castle of Striveling, or Sterling, in Scotland, where a small coin was anciently struck which it is supposed gave the name to all the rest.

We must now explain how a certain weight of gold bullion has come in modern times to be called a pound. The original measure of value in England, France and Scotland was the pound weight of silver bullion. No coin, however, of this actual weight was ever struck. But the pound weight of silver bullion was cut into 240 pieces called pence. Twelve of these pence were called a shilling or solidus; and therefore twenty shillings, or solidi, made a pound. These 240 pence actually weighed a pound of bullion.

Now let us denote the pound weight of metal in the form of bullion by the symbol—lb., and the pound weight of metal in the form of coin by the symbol—£. Then we have—

240 pence = 20 shillings = 1£ = 1 lb.

It is perfectly clear that if the pound weight of bullion were divided into a greater number of pieces than 240, that greater number would still be equal to the pound weight; and if we denoted by the symbol £, 240 pieces or pence, irrespective of their weight, we should have the 1 lb, equal to £1 + the number of pieces above 240.

Now this is what has been done in the coinages of all

the three countries before mentioned. The sovereigns of these countries were frequently in want of money to pursue their various extravagances, and as they could not make more money they adopted the fraudulent and surreptitious plan of cutting the pound weight of bullion into a greater number of pieces, but they still called them by the same name. By this means they gained an illusory augmentation of wealth. As they could not multiply the quantity of the metal, they at various periods falsified the certificate. While they still called them by the same name, they diminished the quantity of bullion in them, and so coined more than the original number of pence out of a pound weight of bullion.

The consequence of this was very manifest, as 240 pence were still called a pound, or £, in money, whatever their weight was, and as more than 240 pence were coined out of a pound weight of bullion, the £, or pound of money in coin, began to vary from the ℔., or pound weight of bullion. Edward I. began this evil practice in 1300, when he coined 243 pence out of the pound weight of bullion. Subsequent sovereigns followed the same evil example; and this falsification of the certificate increased till in the time of Elizabeth no less than 744 pence, or 62 shillings, were coined out of the pound weight of bullion. Then we have manifestly—

744 pence = 62 shillings = £3 2s = 1℔.

As there are twelve ounces in the pound weight of bullion, it is seen that each ounce was coined into sixty-two pence, and hence as the value of bullion is measured by the ounce, the mint price of silver was said to be 5s. 2d. the ounce.

In the reign of Charles II., the African Company brought home a large quantity of gold from the Guinea coast. He had it coined into pieces called guineas, which were intended to represent the £, or twenty shillings in silver. In 1717 Sir Isaac Newton, then Master of the Mint, reported to Parliament that the true value of the guinea according to the relative market value of gold and silver at that time was 20s. 8d. A royal proclamation, however, was issued, declaring them to be current at twenty-one shillings.

Gold and silver coin were then made unlimited legal tender for debts of any amount. Gold gradually became to be considered as the measure of value in England.

Forty pounds weight of standard gold bullion by the regulations of the English mint are cut into 1,869 pounds.

The legal weight of a sovereign or pound is five dwts. $3\frac{17}{623}$ grains, containing $113\frac{1}{623}$ grains of fine gold. Sovereigns which fall below 5 dwts. 2¾ grains, and half-sovereigns of less than 2 dwts. 13½ grains, cease to be legal tender.

It was adopted as a principle of law in 1816 that a nation should adopt only one metal as the legal measure of value, and make any other that may be used subsidiary, and gold coin was declared the only legal tender to an unlimited amount, and the silver and copper coins were intended only as small change for the gold coin.

Banks are usually divided into three classes, as they are merely for the custody or issue of money, or for both.

BANKS OF DEPOSIT.—The first class, or the banks of deposit, are, strictly speaking, those early banks which received money or valuables for custody, and kept them in their coffers till called for; but now the term is generally applied to those establishments that receive money from their customers, and lend it out to others at a higher rate of interest.

BANKS OF ISSUE.—Banks of issue are those that issue their own notes for circulation; but as they likewise receive deposits, the term is generally applied to what forms the third class of the division. Were the duties of banks limited to the safe custody of money, they would still be of immense advantage to the public. Every one who has the care of large sums of money knows the anxiety that attends their custody, and the risks to which they are subjected; and hence the value of a place of security in which to lodge them. This gave rise to the first formation of public banks. But, were the money merely to lie idly in the coffers of the bank, it is evident that the depositor would not only not receive any interest upon it, but would have to pay for the trouble and expense of keeping it; while the money thus kept was so much drawn from the trading capital of the country.

The advantages of combining a system of lending money with that of receiving it soon became apparent; and banks were established for the purpose of both receiving and lending money; the interest received on the sums being considered sufficient to cover all expense connected with its management, or the risk of losing it. By this means, numerous small sums of money, which would have remained unproductive in the hands of individuals, are collected into large sums in the hands of the bankers, who employ it in granting facilities to trade and commerce, and in this way increase the productive capital of the nation. Thus a million of money, in place of lying useless in small sums in the hands of the owners, or in one large sum in the coffers of a bank, is lent out to increase the capital of manufacturers and traders ; and thus the world is made one million richer, or at least is saved from being one million poorer. Besides the money which a banker receives in deposits from his customers, he must be possessed of a certain capital of his own, in order to carry on business ; and to insure confidence in his stability ; for no one would lend money to a banker if he knew that he was possessed of no capital. The interest derived from this capital forms part of the profits of the banker, but it is evident that the profit in this case is not the same as that which he derives from trading with the capital of others ; in other words, that the interest is not greater than if he had lent out his money in any other way equally safe, and involving the same amount of trouble. The deposits over and above a certain sum which he must have at hand to meet daily claims, he advances in various ways as loans. The best and safest mode of employing such funds is considered to be in the discounting of good mercantile bills of exchange; that is, bills representing bona fide transactions of trade and commerce.

In the first place, banks are useful as places of security for the deposit of money. Banking increases the productive capital of a country. Another advantage conferred upon society by bankers is that they make advances to persons who want to borrow money, when proper security is presented. Persons engaged in trade and commerce are thus enabled to augment their capital, and consequently their wealth. The increase of money in circulation stimulates production. When bankers are compelled to withhold their usual accommodation, both the commercial and the agricultural interests are plunged into extreme distress. Banking also exercises a powerful influence upon the morals of society. It tends to produce honesty and punctuality in pecuniary engagements. It is thus that bankers perform the functions of public conservators of the commercial virtues. From motives of private interest they encourage the industrious, the prudent, the punctual, and the honest, while they discountenance the reckless and shiftless business man and speculator. They hold out inducements to uprightness, which are not disregarded by even the most abandoned.

Thompson Hankey, a Director, and formerly Governor of the Bank of England, in his work on the "Principles of Banking," says:—

"We are all destined in this world to earn our bread by the sweat of our brow; and I know no trade or calling in which high religious and moral qualities can be more sensibly appreciated and brought to bear for practical utility in our journey through life than in that of banking. Let me find a man honestly striving to use his best talents and energies in the endeavor to discharge his duties to the best of his ability in that position of life in which it has pleased God to place him—acting as if he were convinced that he can only succeed by living a life based on sound religious principles, which he will never violate for any worldly objects that may appear to tempt him out of his path of duty—and I would infinitely prefer to deal with that man as a banker, or trust him as a correspondent in business with the use of money, than a man of the greatest wealth acquired by less honest means, and acting as if he thought lightly of honesty and integrity. Honesty is a quality which many political economists have thought deserving of at least an equal value as industry and credit; and we who are connected with trade know how immeasurably superior it ought to be esteemed above every other qualification for a good man of business. The old adage that 'honesty is the best policy,' should be prominently placed up in the office of every banking establishment, and should be engraved on the mind of every one who wishes to obtain credit amongst capitalists."

We propose to describe, in a condensed form, some of the most prominent and other banking projects which for half a century occupied public attention, and made the task of founding the Bank of England comparatively easy to the projectors. Many "charity banks" and Lombards, or Lombard-houses, now commonly called pawn brokers, were projected.

"The making transferable all promissory notes between man and man," was recommended by William Potter in his "Key of Wealth."

One Henry Robinson ardently advocated the creation of a Land Bank in which all payments above twenty pounds should be made in bank credit; and that beside the principal bank in London, there should be one hundred subordinate banks in different parts of England, all centering in the said capital bank of London, wherein, for the support of the credit thereof, a general mortgage of lands was proposed, for which the mortgagor should have credit in bank to the value of his land. The condition of such mortgage should be, either to pay so much money, with interest at six per cent. within a year from the day that bank credit should any way fail to be current, or, in default of such payment, the said mortgaged lands to be forfeited without redemption and to be divided amongst the proprietors of the credit in bank. Others proposed a general register of houses and ships as well as of land; a court of merchants for the summary recovery of all debts; also some very ill-judged projects for uniting into corporations all merchants trading into any one country, for the sake of what they call "uniformity of trade."

Samuel Lamb, one of the most eminent London merchants at the time of Charles the First, warmly espoused the subject of public banks, and during the commonwealth presented an "humble address to his Highness the Lord Protector," wherein he described the great advantages the Hollanders derived from banks, and the disadvantages England labored under in their absence. The following reasons, which were embodied in the petition, appear to us to be so prophetic as to deserve to be recorded:—

"The good that we may do ourselves by banks, if settled in England, are many; for no nation ever made use of them but they flourished and thrived accordingly.

"Imprimis: they will, by well ordering them, bring back the gold and silver which hath been drained out of this land by the Hollanders' banks, and by other princes raising the value thereof in their dominions.

"They will much increase the stock of this land, which will wonderfully increase all manner of trade, and will bring in that excellent transferring trade, and make England the staple of all foreign commodities, as Holland is at this time, and has been since they had the use of banks, who have nothing considerable of their own growth and manufactures, yet have the staple of all commerce, as a rich treasure in money and jewels, all materials for shipping, and even all manner of clothing, and the granary and vineyard of Europe, with which commodities they furnish most countries, and which England may also do.

"They will increase and much encourage the fishery of this nation, and breed up in that employment many thousands of seamen, which will find employment in the East Indies' Streights, and other voyages into other parts of the world.

"They will increase the warlike trading, shipping and mariners of this nation, which will much strengthen us against our enemies.

"They will also much increase the revenues and customs of the land by increasing credit.

"They will wonderfully employ the poor of this land, and increase the natural manufacture thereof, and make us capable to buy or sell at home or abroad.

"They will make the English capable to engross the commodity of any country, and withhold it from another that may be at enmity with us to whom the said commodity may be useful to our prejudice, and also make our own price of it.

"They will increase trade in our plantations, and cause ships to be built in New England as good or better than any built in Holland.

"They will furnish factors in England with credit to pay customs and charges of a great cargo of goods, which may on a sudden be conveyed to them; for many times such English factors may be of good estate and credit, yet have not always a great cash lying by them for such uses, though the Dutch are seldom without it; therefore may oftentimes be forced to strain their credit to take up money at interest, or sell all or part of such goods at under-rate for want thereof, which may be a great prejudice to themselves and loss to their principals, and is believed causes many such great commissions to be carried from the English and consigned to the Dutch residing in England, to their great benefit and advantage, and loss and prejudice to the English nation.

"They will increase trade in Ireland, which will people that island, and increase the revenue thereof.

"They will furnish many young men with stock that have by their industry and well-spent time, and travels in their apprenticeships, gained good experience in foreign traffic.

"They will preserve many good men from failing and losing their credit, and many others, which trial and experience will daily discover; as quick and easy paying bills of exchange, foreign or domestic, and all other payments; preventing fraudulent payments in counterfeit or clipt coin or mis-telling money; rectifying errors in accounts which occasion law suits; preventing theft and breaking open houses where money is suspected to be; and robbing in the highways graziers, carriers, or others that used to carry money from fairs and other places, which may be returned by assignment in bank. Whereas now the several hundreds in many places are forced to guard such as carry money for fear of their being robbed, and such hundreds paying them the money they lost, as it hath often fallen out of late time.

"Lastly, a bank with a certain number of sufficient men of estate and credit, joined together in a joint stock, being as it were the general cashkeepers or treasurers of the place where they are settled, and divers others, tending much to the tranquility of your highness and the welfare of the English nation, which, with your highness's favourable encouragement, I shall in all humility be ready to make known to you, and remove any objections as can be alleged in the premises, and propound a way how it may be effected, and the evils remedied and prevented, being unwilling to bury the talent in a napkin which it hath pleased the Giver of all blessings in His great goodness and mercy to bestow upon me, hoping that I shall not offend by tendering this with my best services to your highness."

It appears by the Rolls of Parliament, that, two years after the presentation of the above address to Cromwell, Samuel Lamb petitioned the House of Commons on the subject of his proposal for a bank; and that on Friday, the 4th of March, 1658, the petition was referred to a committee; but it does not subsequently appear that any report was made thereon, or any steps taken to forward his views.

In the year 1651, there appeared the following "Humble Proposal to the honorable Council of Trade, and all Merchants and others who desire to improve their Estates," which, if enacted by Parliament, "would, as with due submission is conceived, conduce to advance trade, employ the poor, diminish interest, improve public revenue, prevent the cruelty of creditors and the injustice of debtors, tending likewise speedily to promote the enterprise discovered in a late treatise, entitled 'The Key of Wealth.'"

This proposal had reference to a bank of credit, in which bills of exchange were to be the principal circulating medium.

In the year 1665, a very elaborate account of the "Office of Credit" appeared. The author endeavors to remove what he calls two vulgar errors, viz: "That credit in bank is only current because men can have money when they will;" and further "that without money no trade can be managed." At the end of the work there is a summary of the whole; the author's main object, as he himself states, is satisfactorily to answer the objections, "that men will have money and not credit."

Scheme followed scheme for the establishment of a solid bank, but none met with royal favor and aid from Parliament until William Paterson made public his plans for the Bank of England, which is described at length in the following chapter.

CHAPTER III.

FOUNDATION AND EARLY HISTORY OF THE BANK OF ENGLAND.

Why the Bank was Established—Origin of the Bank—The Governor and Company of the Bank of England—History of William Paterson, its Founder—He dies Unhonored and Neglected—Prophets who Predicted Financial Ruin—"The Old Lady of Threadneedle Street"—Paterson and his Ill-Fated Darien Scheme—Present Condition of the Bank—The Policy of the Bank Assailed by the Public—How the Bank is Officered—The Bank Charter—How it Reads—Restrictions, Impositions and Demands—Buying Property from and Lending Money to the Crown—Suspending Payment of Notes—Assistance from the Government Averts a Failure—Capital Increased—Confidence Restored—Length of Original Charter.

THE important position assumed by England towards the middle of the seventeenth century, rendered the absence of a national bank somewhat surprising. The nation was rapidly increasing in commercial and political greatness, and although several projects were issued for banks, the necessity for their formation not being absolutely felt the proposals were dismissed without much attention.

There were many reasons for the establishment of a national bank. It was necessary for the sake of a secure paper currency. It was required for the support of the national credit and reducing the rate of interest. In 1546, the payment of interest had been rendered legal, and fixed at ten per cent. In 1624 the rate was reduced to eight per cent. The rate of interest, which was higher in England than abroad, rendered trade comparatively disadvantageous to England.

Sixteen years previous to the establishment of the Bank of England, proposals and schemes for a national bank were discussed, but none were considered practicable, although one or two were tried.

A very curious account of the origin of the Bank of England is to be found in a pamphlet printed in 1717, called the "Conferences on the Public Debts, by the Wednesday's Club in Friday Street." The discussions among the members of this society excited considerable public attention; William Paterson, who was evolving a scheme for a bank, belonged to this club, the members of which presented a petition to King William, setting forth among other things the great advantages of a public bank—but at that time their proposal was received with suspicion.

Paterson anticipated that the government would readily incorporate, with certain powers and privileges, such parties as would advance a considerable sum of money by way of loan to meet the public exigencies. Yet, as he himself relates in the account of his transactions in relation to the Bank of England, printed in 1695, that he found it much more difficult to get it consented to by the Privy Council, in order to be brought into Parliament, than he had at first apprehended.

The Bank of England, which has long been the principal bank of deposit and circulation in Great Britain, and indeed in Europe, was founded in 1694. The government being at that time much distressed for money, brought about in great measure from the defects and abuses in the system of taxation, and partly from the difficulty of borrowing money on account of the supposed instability of the government, the Bank of England actually grew out of a loan to the government of £1,200,000 for the public service. The subscribers, besides receiving eight per cent. on the sum advanced as interest, and £4,000 a year as the expense of management, in all £100,000 a year, were incorporated into a society denominated the "Governor and Company of the Bank of England." Many consider that to the war with France, and the extreme difficulty the government experienced in raising funds for the conduct of the war, is the institution of this giant monopoly due. The idea of the Bank of England originated solely with William Paterson, a merchant of London, a brainy Scotchman. Paterson readily saw that the government, which had been paying interest at the rate of from 20 to 40 per cent. per annum, would, without much hesitation, grant exclusive and almost unlimited privileges to such parties as would in turn furnish it with a fixed and permanent loan, at a reasonable rate of interest. The plan, being brought to the attention of the

King, was submitted to the Privy Council, when the details were completed, and it was laid before Parliament. Here it met with the violent opposition of a formidable party. Nevertheless, the bill was finally carried by the government, and on April 25, 1694, became a law, from which date the original charter was granted for eleven years.

Of William Paterson, the author of the Bank of England, but little is known. It is perhaps unfortunate that no biography of this remarkable man exists. As the projector of the Bank of England, he deserves notice. He was born in Traillflat, Scotland, in 1658, and was educated for the ministry. A speculative, as well as an adventurous man, he was the soul of the ill-fated Darien expedition, and losing all returned to England to die neglected, unhonored and ignored by his former business associates.

The name of the founder of the Bank of England was not upon the list of directors only for the year of its establishment in 1694. The facts which led to his departure from the honored part of director are difficult to learn; but it is not at all improbable that Paterson was too daring and speculative for those with whom he was joined in companionship. One writer says: "The friendless Scot was tricked out of the post and the honors he had earned." Sir John Dalrymple remarks: "The persons to whom Paterson applied made use of his ideas, took the honor and credit to themselves, and absolutely neglected him afterwards."

Paterson found it more difficult to procure consent than he anticipated, and all those who feared an invasion of their interests were arrayed against it. The goldsmith foresaw the destruction of his monopoly, and he opposed it from self interest. The Tory foresaw an easier mode of gaining money for the government he approved. The usurer foresaw the destruction of his oppressive extortion, and he resisted it with the vigor of his craft. The rich man foresaw his profits diminished on government contracts, and he vehemently and virtuously opposed it on public principles. The outcries were hard and long, but to no avail. Prophets are in their graves who predicted the early downfall of the Bank of England. The supporters claimed that the bank would rescue the nation out of the hands of extortioners, lower interest, raise the value of land, renew public credit, extend circulation, improve commerce, and connect the people more closely with the government.

As previously stated there were many reasons why a national bank should be established. To relieve the moneyless government was one of the objects of the founder of the Bank of England, and though his motive was not wholly unselfish nor unconditionally patriotic; though he was bitterly opposed and relentlessly assailed by usurers, shylocks and others who had profited by extortionate discounts and the general helplessness of the government, and by a large and demonstrative class who declared that such a bank would at once become a dangerous monopoly, and engross the whole money of the kingdom, and that it would be arbitrary in its powers; but the indomitable William Paterson not only obtained a charter, but was very soon justified in affirming that the bank had spared the ministers their humiliating processions into London to secure loans at ten and twelve per cent. interest; given life and currency to double or treble the value of its capital in other branches of public credit; and it was patent to all that the bank was the principal means of the success of the campaign in 1695, particularly in reducing Namur, the first step towards the peace of 1697.

This man, William Paterson, who founded the Bank of England, and also the Bank of Scotland, was a dreamer of a lofty and generous nature and large ideas, which sometimes carried him into the impracticable, though usually there was a substratum of utility to what seemed to be the least substantial of his schemes. It was Paterson who led the Darien expedition, that wild attempt to establish another East India Company and to found an Arcadia on the American isthmus. On the 26th of July, 1698, four years after the establishment of the bank, twelve hundred persons, many of whom were of high birth and influence, embarked with Paterson from Leith, and in due time reached the site of their proposed colony. Paterson had purchased the land from its Indian possessors, and proclaimed as the two leading principles of his commonwealth: freedom of faith and freedom of trade to all sects and to all nations. His generosity was unbounded, and when the colony seemed most likely to succeed, he voluntarily surrendered the large share of the profits which belonged to him.

The adventurers were first charmed with their new home, but their subsequent fate was something deplorable. They fell victims to famine, disease and the attacks of the Spaniards. Utopia was once again laid waste, and of the number which left Leith only thirty ever again set foot in their native land. One of these was Paterson, of whom a letter of the period said: "The colonists give him due praise, for he hath been diligent and true to the end."

The chivalrous and high-minded man was followed by misfortune. The persons to whom he applied made use of his ideas; were civil to him for awhile and then absolutely neglected him. Paterson was a man prolific of good ideas but utterly unable to direct them for his own gain. He always took scheming men into his confidence, which of course ruined him.

The Act of Parliament by which the bank was established, is entitled: "An Act for granting to their Majesties, several duties upon tonnage of ships and vessels, and upon beer, ale and other liquors, for securing certain recompenses and advantages in the said Act mentioned, to such persons as shall voluntarily advance the sum of £1,500,000 towards carrying on the war with France." After a variety of enactments relative to "the duty upon tonnage of ships and vessels, and upon beer, ale, and other liquors," the Act authorizes the raising of £1,200,000 by voluntary subscription, the subscribers to be formed into a corporation, and be styled: "The Governor and Company of the Bank of England." The sum of £300,000 was also to be raised by subscription, and the contributors, of which there were but 1,300, to receive instead, annuities for one, two, or three lives. Towards the £1,200,000 no one person was to subscribe more than £10,000 before the first day of July next ensuing, nor at any time more than £20,000. The corporation were to lend their whole capital to the Government, for which they were to receive interest at the rate of 8 per cent. per annum, and £4,000 per annum for management; being £100,000 per annum in the whole. They were not allowed to borrow or owe more than the amount of their capital; and if they did so, the individual members became liable to the creditors, in proportion to the amount of their stock. They were not to trade in any "goods, wares, or merchandise whatsoever;" but they were allowed to deal in bills of exchange, gold or silver bullion, and to sell any goods, wares, or merchandise, upon which they had advanced money, and which had not been redeemed within three months after the time agreed upon. The whole subscription having been filled in ten days, a charter was issued on the 27th day of July, 1694. The management of the corporation was intrusted to a Governor, a Deputy Governor, and twenty-four directors, all elected annually, and all subjects of England, the Governor being required to have at least £4,000 of the capital stock of the bank in his own name, the Deputy Governor at least £3,000, and each Director £2,000. When the subscription was complete the sum was handed into the Exchequer, and the bank procured from other quarters the funds which it required for the transaction of its current business.

The current business at the foundation of the bank was not large, and all of it was done in one medium sized room. To-day it is the most extensive banking institution in the world. It employs over one thousand clerks, and its buildings cover over eight acres of ground. But from its inception to the present day it has manifestly held up its head through all vicissitudes, and has been inseparably connected with the fortunes of the English government. At times it has been a supplicant, then a dictator, nurtured by Halifax, bullied by Walpole and coaxed by Pitt. If it has not always been generous in times of adversity, it has been prudent, and its influence has been against chimeras and reckless speculation; and because it has not in all seasons of commercial distress been willing to play the part of benefactor, it has been assailed by scribblers and disappointed men to such an extent that the titles of their choleric outbreaks cover some thirty pages of the British Museum Catalogue.

"The Old Lady of Threadneedle Street," a cant name for the Bank of England, which is situated in Threadneedle street, is a synonym of strength and security throughout the civilized world. Its notes are as good as gold in any community, and a Bank of England note stands at par in the wilds of Africa even as it does in the City of London. This institution is regarded with pride, not only by the English but by every man or woman who speaks that language, and is regarded with awe and reverence by financiers and intelligent people in all parts of the world.

The present capital and surplus of the Bank of England is $86,704,781. The capital is £14,553,000. £16,200,000 is now issued by the bank on securities. Debt of the government to the bank is £11,015,100; the bank also holds government securities for £5,184,900. Shares of Bank of England are worth £315. The dividends for the year ending Oct. 5, 1888, were at the rate of 9¾ per cent.

On the first of January, 1695, the bank commenced active operations, although open and preparing for work since the preceding July.

On the 19th of January, same year, a petition from

several merchants and traders of the city of London, on behalf of themselves and others, was presented to the House of Commons, setting forth:—"That by an Act made the last session of this Parliament, for granting to their Majesties a duty upon the tonnage of ships, etc., and by virtue of their Majesties' letters patent in pursuance of the said Act, a corporation of the Governor and Company of the Bank of England is established to receive and manage the sum of £1,200,000; which said bank, as the same is and may be managed, is ruinous and destructive to trade in general, injurious to his Majesty's revenues, prejudicial to the lands and manufactures of this nation, and is only a private advantage to the said corporation."

This petition was taken into consideration on January 22, 1695, when the petitioners, together with the governor and directors of the bank, attended the House of Commons, and were informed that their petition could not be received. This decision of the House of Commons was considered conclusive as to the degree of protection which the bank might calculate upon receiving from the government; but it had the effect of causing the publication of sharp and bitter animadversions upon its management, and of the retirement of several of the directors.

In granting the charter for the Bank of England, Parliament declared amongst other things, that the management shall be "capable in law, to purchase, enjoy, and retain to them and their successors, any moneys, lands, rents, tenements, and possessions whatsoever; and to purchase and acquire all sorts of goods and chattels whatsoever, wherein they are not restrained by Act of Parliament; and also to grant, demise, and dispose of the same.

"That the management and government of the corporation be committed to the governor and twenty-four directors, who shall be elected between the 25th of March and the 25th of April of each year, from among the members of the company duly qualified.

"That no dividend shall at any time be made by the said governor and company, save only out of the interest, profit, or produce arising by, or out of the said capital stock, or fund, or by such dealing as is allowed by Act of Parliament.

"The governor, deputy governor and directors must be natural born subjects of England; or naturalized subjects; they shall have in their own name and for their own use capital stock of the Bank of England to the following amount: The governor, at least £4,000, deputy governor £3,000, and director £2,000.

"That thirteen or more of the said governors and directors (of which the governor or deputy governor must be always one), shall constitute a court of directors, for the management of the affairs of the company, and for the appointment of all agents and servants which may be necessary, paying them such salaries as they may consider reasonable.

"Every elector must have, in his own name and for his own use, £500 or more capital stock, and can only give one vote. He must, if required by any member present, take the oath of stock, or the declaration of stock, in case he may be one of the people called Quakers.

"Four general courts shall be held in every year, in the month of September, December, April and July. A general court may be summoned at any time, upon the requisition of nine proprietors duly qualified as electors. The majority of electors in general courts have the power to make and constitute by-laws and ordinances for the government of the corporation, provided that such by-laws and ordinances be not repugnant to the laws of the Kingdom."

Armed with this authority from the government, the Bank of England commenced business on July 27, 1694. The applications for stock in the new enterprise were numerous, and the projectors were thereby enabled to select first-class men for stockholders and officers. The bank immediately issued notes, none of which were, however, of a smaller denomination than £20 sterling, and commenced discounting bills of exchange at rates varying from 3 to 6 per cent., distinction being made in favor of persons who used the bank as a place of deposit.

The Bank of England had not issued any notes for less than £20 previously to 1759, when it commenced the issue of £10 notes; but the country bankers put in circulation notes for such small sums that Parliament enacted in 1775, that none should be issued for less than £1. In 1777 this minimum limit was further raised to £5, but in spite of this restriction the number and the amount of the issues of the country bankers soon became dangerously multiplied.

The Bank of England is prohibited by law from engaging in any sort of commercial undertaking, other than dealing in bills of exchange, and gold and silver. It is authorized to advance money upon the security of goods or merchandise pledged to it, and to sell by public auction such goods as are not redeemed within a specified time.

There was virtually no end of Parliamentary tinkering with the new bank, and in the latter part of the year the corporation was organized it was enacted by statute that "the bank shall not deal in any goods, wares, or merchandise (except bullion), or purchase any lands or revenues belonging to the Crown, or advance, or lend to their Majesties, their heirs or successors, any sum or sums of money, by way of loan or anticipation on any part or parts, branch or branches, fund or funds of the revenue, now granted or belonging, or hereafter to be granted to their Majesties, their heirs and successors, other than such fund or funds, part or parts, branch or branches of the said revenue only on which a credit of loan is, or shall be granted by Parliament." The foregoing Parliamentary injunction interfered with a profitable business the bank had built up with certain titled dignitaries.

In 1697 the government caused to have enacted a bill that was regarded with great favor by the bank. It was, "that the common capital, or the principal stock of the Bank of England, and also the real fund of the Governor and Company, or any profit or produce to be made thereof, or arising thereby, shall be exempted from any rates, taxes, assessments, or impositions whatsoever during the continuance of the bank; that all the profit, benefit and advantage from time to time arising out of the management of the said corporation, shall be applied to the uses of all the members of the said association of the Governor and Company of the Bank of England, ratably and in proportion to each members' part, share, and interest in the common capital and principal stock of the said Governor and Company hereby established."

In 1696, during the great recoinage, the bank was involved in numerous difficulties, and was even compelled to suspend payment of its notes, which had fallen as low as 20 per cent. below par. Owing, however, to the judicious conduct of the directors, and the prompt assistance of the government, the bank got over the crisis. Had it not been for the aid of the government the bank would have succumbed to the strain and passed out of existence. It was at this time judged expedient, in order to place it in a situation the better to withstand any adverse circumstances that might afterwards occur, to immediately increase the capital from £1,200,000 to £2,201,171. This increase inspired confidence with the public in the integrity, solvency and judicious management of the bank, which evinced itself in many ways. The increase in capital, among other things, had the effect within a few months of causing the stock not only to recover a discount of from 40 to 50 per cent. but to sell at a premium of 12 per cent.

The charter of the Bank of England enumerates at some length the fundamental principles of the corporation, and displays in the manner in which it is drawn up, a considerable extent of knowledge of commercial affairs. Instead, however, of obtaining exclusive privileges of trading, which a century before would have been an object of ambition with a society of merchants, the bank was restricted to the dealing in bills of exchange and in gold and silver. It was prohibited from taking part in any mercantile concern; but it was authorized to make advances on the security of merchandise lodged with it, or pledged to it by written documents. The latter description of business, it was thought, would form the principal source of profit. The wisdom of the founders of the bank has long since been apparent, but William Paterson, who was the originator and prime mover in its organization, was brushed aside by unscrupulous associates and dethroned of the honor really due him. The Bank of England, however, stands to-day a monument to Paterson's greatness.

CHAPTER IV.

HISTORY OF RENEWALS, DEBTS, AND PANICS.

Advancing Money to the Government—How the Bank Receives Pay from the Government—Persecution—The "Dead Weight"—Table of Renewals of Charter, with Capital, Debt and Conditions of Renewals—An Explanation by an Ex-Governor of the Bank—Amount of Loans to the Government—Present Capital of the Bank of England—A Panic Quieted by a Novel Method—Merchants Come to the Bank's Rescue—The Bank Attacked by Rioters—Solidity of the Bank of England.

THE charter of the Bank of England, when first granted in 1694, was to continue for eleven years certain, or till a year's notice after the first of August, 1705.

The charter was further prolonged in 1697. In 1708, the bank having advanced £400,000 for the public service, without interest, the exclusive privileges of the corporation were prolonged till 1733. And in consequence of various advances made at different times, the exclusive privileges of the bank have been continued, with the proviso that they might be cancelled on a year's notice.

In addition to the permanent debt of the government to the bank, the latter contracted with the former on March 20, 1823, to pay at stated intervals between 1823 and 1828 certain pensions and annuities arising out of the then recent wars, amounting to £13,089,419. This is termed the "dead weight." In consideration of this the bank was to receive from the government an annuity of £585,740 for 44 years.

Although the necessities of the State contributed to the establishment of the Bank of England, they were, at intervals of every few years, compelled, after making a feeble resistance, to purchase the continuance of the privileges on exceedingly onerous terms. The history of the seven renewals of the charter between 1694 and 1800, and of the accordance of permission to increase the capital of the bank, is one continuous record of exactions.

The bank, as a condition of State patronage, was on each successive occasion forced to increase its loans to the Government at low rates of interest or without any interest whatever, three millions sterling being lent for six years without interest in 1800. Interest on previous loans was reduced, exchequer bills were cancelled, and on one occasion a free gift of £110,000 was made to the State. As a consequence the Government debt to the bank increased at a rapid rate, till it amounted at last to upwards of fourteen and a half millions sterling, or rather more than the whole capital of the corporation. In 1833 the Government paid off one-fourth of this debt in reduced annuities, and thereby reduced it to £11,015,100, at which amount it now stands. While Ministry after Ministry thus accurately tested the pliability of the "Governor and Company," and relentlessly preyed on their fears as to the continuance of their monopoly, an intense feeling of loyalty actuated the directors in all their dealings with the State. When, after the Rebellion in 1715, the Government proposed to reduce the interest on the National Debt from six to five per cent., the bank testified to their desire to assist the measure by at once agreeing to accept the lower rate, and to provide money to pay off those creditors who declined to submit to the reduction. Again, when a further reduction in the interest on part of the National Debt was proposed in 1750, the bank at once assented, and arranged to find a sum of money to pay off the dissentients.

The following table of renewals should be carefully noted. It gives an account of the successive renewals of the charter, of the conditions under which these renewals were made, and of the variations in the amount and interest of the permanent debt due by Government to the bank, exclusive of the "dead weight:"—

Date of Renewal.	Conditions under which Renewals were made and Permanent Debt contracted.	Permanent Debt.
		£. s. d.
1694	Charter granted redeemable upon the expiration of 12 months' notice after the first of August, 1705, upon payment by the public to the bank of the demand therein specified. Under the Act the bank advanced to the Government £1,200,000 in consideration of their receiving an annuity of £100,000 a year, viz: 8 per cent. interest and £4,000 for management...	1,200,000 0 0
1697	Charter continued by 8 and 9 Will. III. c. 20, till twelve months' notice after 1st of August, 1710, on payment, &c. Under this Act the bank took up and added to their stock £1,001,171 Exchequer bills and tallies.	
1708	Charter continued by 7 Anne, c. 7, till twelve months' notice after 1st of August, 1732, on payment &c. Under this Act the bank	

Date of Renewal.	Conditions under which Renewals were made and Permanent Debt contracted.	Permanent Debt.
		£ s. d.
	advanced £400,000 to Government without interest, and delivered up to be cancelled £1,775,027, 17s. 10d. Exchequer bills, in consideration of their receiving an annuity of £106,501, 13s., being at the rate of 6 per cent....................	2,175,027 17 10
1713	Charter continued by 12 Anne, stat. 1, c. 11, till twelve months' notice after the 1st of August, 1742, on payment, &c.	
	In 1716, by the 3 Geo. I. c. 8 the bank advanced to Government, at 5 per cent....	2,000,000 0 0
	And by the same Act the interest on the Exchequer bills cancelled in 1780 was reduced from 6 to 5 per cent.	
	In 1721, by 8 Geo. I. c. 21, the South Sea Company was authorized to sell £200,000 Government annuities, and corporations purchasing the same at 26 years' purchase were authorized to add the	

Date of Renewal.	Conditions under which Renewals were made and Permanent Debt contracted.	Permanent Debt.
	amount to their capital stock. The bank purchased the whole of these annuities at twenty years, purchase..	£ s. d. 4,000,000 0 0
	Five per cent. interest was payable on this sum to midsummer 1727, and thereafter 4 per cent.	9,375,027 17 10
	At different times between 1727 and 1738, both inclusive, the bank received from the public, on account of permanent debt, £3,275,027, 17s. 10d., and advanced to it, on account of ditto, £3,000,000: Difference....	275,027 17 10
	Debt due by the public in 1738....................	9,100,000 0 0
1742	Charter continued by 15 Geo. II. c. 13, till 12 months' notice after the 1st of August, 1764, on payment, &c. Under this Act the bank advanced £1,600,000 without interest, which, being added to the original advance of £1,200,000, and the £400,000 advanced in 1710,	

Date of Renewal	Conditions under which Renewals were made and Permanent Debt contracted.	Permanent Debt.
	bearing interest at 6 per cent., reduced the interest on the whole to 3 per cent..	£ s. d 1,600,000 0 0
	In 1745, under authority of 19 Geo. II. c. 6, the bank delivered up to be cancelled £986,000 of Exchequer bills, in consideration of an annuity of £39,472, being at the rate of 3 per cent....	986,000 0 0
1764	In 1749, the 23d Geo. II. c. 6, reduced the interest on the 4 per cent. annuities, held by the bank, to 3½ per cent. for seven years from the 25th of December, 1750, and thereafter to 3 per cent. Charter continued by 4 Geo III. c. 25, till twelve months' notice after the 1st of August 1786, on payment, &c.	
1781	Under this Act the bank paid into the Exchequer £110,000, free of all charge. Charter continued by 21 Geo. III. c. 60, till twelve months' notice after the 1st of August, 1812, on payment, &c.	

BANK OF ENGLAND.

Date of Renewal	Conditions under which Renewals were made and Permanent Debt contracted.	Permanent Debt.		
		£	s.	d.
1800	Under this Act the bank advanced £30,000,000 for the public service for three years, at 3 per cent. Charter continued by 40 Geo. III. c. 28, till twelve months' notice after the 1st of August, 1833, on payment, &c.			
	Under this Act the bank advanced to Government £3,000,000 for six years without interest; but in pursuance of the recommendation of the committee of 1807, the advance was continued, without interest, till six months after the signature of a definitive treaty of peace.			
	In 1816, the bank, under authority of the Act 56 Geo. III. c. 96, advanced at 3 per cent., to be repaid on or before the 1st of August, 1833.	3,000,000	0	0
1833	Charter continued by 3 and 4 Will. IV. c. 98, till twelve months' notice after the 1st of August, 1855, with a pro-	14,686,000	0	0

Date of Renewal.	Conditions under which Renewals were made and Permanent Debt contracted.	Permanent Debt.
		£. s. d.
	viso that it may be dissolved on twelve months' notice after the 1st of August, 1855, on payment, &c.	
	This Act directs that in future the bank shall deduct £120,000 a year from their charge on account of the management of the public debt; and that a fourth part of the debt due by the public to the bank, or £3,671,000, be paid off..........	3,671,000 0 0
	Permanent advance by the bank to the public, bearing interest at 3 per cent., independent of the advances on account of dead weight, or other public securities held by it...............	11,015,000 0 0
1844	Charter continued by 7 and 8 Vict. c. 32, till twelve mos. after the 1st of August, 1855, on payment, &c.	
	This act exempts the notes of the bank from all charge on account of stamp-duty, and directs that in	

Date of Renewal.	Conditions under which Renewals were made and Permanent Debt contracted.	Permanent Debt.
	future the bank shall deduct a further sum of £180,000 a year from the charge on account of the management of the public debt. It also allows notes of the value of £14,000,000 to be issued on securities, separates the banking from the issuing department of the establishment, and effects other important changes. The amount now issued on securities (October, 1898,) is £16,200,000. Present debt of the Government to the bank (1888) is £11,015,100.	£ s. d.

In 1861, a fresh arrangement was made between the government and the bank, to endure for twenty-five years, and under this agreement the bank receives £300 per million on £600,000,000, and £150 per million on the amount of debt above that sum; but from these allowances are deducted £60,000 for exemption from stamp duties and the whole allowance out of profit of issue, making together nearly £200,000. Charter will continue until the bank gives the government twelve months' notice and by the payment of all public debts—but notice has not yet been given, nor is it contemplated.

Many people imagine that the government and the bank are so closely identified, one with the other, that it would be impossible to separate their interests ; but this is a great mistake. The government, although debtors to the bank, are in every other respect perfectly independent of that corporation : and indeed, the debt is of such a nature that it cannot be called in but on certain conditions, a consideration having been given for the loan of the money ; which consideration, as we have before shown, consists in the privilege of being bankers to the State, and the sole bank of issue under certain conditions previously mentioned.

By referring to the preceding table of renewals it will be noted that the capital of the bank on which dividends are paid have never exactly coincided with, though it has seldom differed very materially from, the permanent advance by the bank to the government. We have already seen that it amounted, in 1708, to £4,402,342. Between that year and 1727, it had increased to near £9,000,000. In 1746 it amounted to £10,780,000. From this period it underwent no change till 1782, when it was increased 8 per cent., amounting to £11,642,400. It continued stationary at this sum down to 1816, when it was raised to £14,553,000, by an addition of 25 per cent. from the profits of the bank. In 1833, the Act for the renewal of the charter directed that the sum of £3,671,700, being the fourth part of the debt due by the government to the bank, should be paid to the latter, giving the bank the option of deducting it from its capital. But that has not been done ; and after sundry changes, the capital of the Bank of England amounts to-day as formerly, to £14,553,000, or seventy-three millions of dollars. The reserve is £3,414,660.

In the year 1844 Parliament passed the Bank Charter Act, which separated the issue from the banking department, and placed the note issue upon its present basis. The extensions of its corporate existence, noted at the beginning of this chapter, were not always voluntarily granted, but were the occasion of bitter controversy, and were dearly paid for. Over and over the bank accommodated the government, and sometimes accommodations were wrung from it as a condition of the continuance of its existence.

Up to 1844 the Bank of England, and private banks out of London with not more than six partners, could issue any number of notes, the "promise to pay" on the face of which was guaranteed only by the desire and ability of the issuers to keep faith with the holders of them; but by the act of that year all banks established subsequently were prohibited from issuing notes, and the issue of banks then existing was limited. In the case of the Bank of England the same Act, in separating the issue department from the banking department, defined the limits within which the issue of notes upon securities must be confined, and provided that the bank should purchase any amount of gold offered to it at a certain fixed rate, or, in other words, receive in deposit any quantity at a certain rate in exchange for notes. Since 1844 the governors and directors of the corporation have had practically no control over the issue of the notes, that is the Act providing that any excess of issue above £14,000,000 (now, October, 1888, £16,000,000) represented by securities shall have its equivalent in bullion.

Some may wonder, perhaps, how it would be possible

to pay all notes in gold when £15,000,000 of them are not represented by gold in possession of the bank, but by securities. The method has been thus lucidly explained by Thomson Hankey, Esq., an ex-governor and one of the directors of the bank. Supposing that all the notes outstanding, except the £15,000,000, were presented for payment, there would be enough gold in the bank to meet them at any hour of any day, and long before the funds could be reduced to fifteen millions.

By any legal process the bank would begin to realize on the £15,000,000 of securities. Four millions of the securities are of a class salable at all times, and the remaining £11,000,000 are loaned to the government. If there should be any need of that sum, the Chancellor of the Exchequer would have no difficulty in turning the government's debt to the bank into three-per-cent. stock, which he would assign to the governor and company, and they would sell the stock as required, receiving in payment their own notes, which would be immediately cancelled.

The good luck that has always attended the bank has become proverbial, and it has become customary to hear people say, when desiring to convey an idea of solidity or reliability: "As sound as the Bank of England." However, the bank has been frequently affected by panics among the holders of her notes. In 1745 the alarm occasioned by the advance of the Highlanders, under the Pretender, as far as Derby, led to a run upon the bank. The streets about the bank were thronged with an angry and excited crowd, the major portion of them being attracted through curiosity, and as the throng augmented the noise and confusion became greater, and rumors of failure were sent flying to all parts of London. The managers were equal to the occasion, and in order to gain time to effect measures for allaying the unwarranted excitement and to effect measures for averting the run, it was decided to adopt the device of paying in shillings and sixpences; but they derived a more effectual relief from the retreat of the Highlanders, and also from a resolution agreed to at a meeting of the leading merchants and traders of London, and very numerously signed, asserting their belief in the solvency and future of the bank, and declaring their willingness to receive the bills of the bank from any person in payment of any sum that might be due to them, and also pledging themselves to use their utmost endeavors to make all their payments in the same medium.

In June, 1780, the bank was attacked by rioters, but no damage was incurred. A considerable military force guards the bank every night as a protection in any emergency that may occur.

The Bank of England is known, and has long been known, to possess the largest capital of any bank in the world, it being at present, 1888, £14,553,000, with a reserve fund of £3,414,660. The prestige it has always enjoyed is very great. No government has ever questioned its security for public deposits of all kinds. The stock has become a favorite investment for public, private, and trust funds; and it is very questionable whether it would enjoy the same reputation with a greatly diminished capital. The shareholders do not complain, and there certainly can be no reason why any one else should desire a change.

But it would be an error to conclude that the capital

of the bank is not so invested as to be of use to the trading community. The amounts lent to corporations for local improvements, to railways on their debentures, and in various other ways, all tend to relieve the money market from a certain number of applicants, and thus more capital is left free for other commercial requirements.

The bank has always been in a position to meet all the legitimate claims upon it from its own depositors, and all these depositors could be paid off and the bank wound up and brought to a conclusion within a very few months, without its being required to touch one farthing of the capital, which would thus remain for division amongst its proprietors.

CHAPTER V.

PROGRESS OF BANKING.

The Desirability of a National Bank—Success Brings Competition—The Scheme for a "National Land Bank."—Country Banks Issue their Own Notes—War for Independence in America—Great Industrial and Commercial Development—Startling Increase in Banks—Unreliable Bankers, Worthless Paper, Unlimited Credit and Prodigal Bankers Precipitate a Big Crash—Violent Revulsion in London—300 out of 350 Banks Compelled to Stop Payments—The Bank Assailed by Jealous Competitors—Its Triumph—Given Exclusive Banking Privileges—Banks Prohibited from Doing Business Within Sixty-five Miles of London—Sir Henry Parnell on Banking.

PREVIOUS to the establishment of the Bank of England much of the nation's spare money was deposited with the goldsmiths, and the receipts they issued circulated from hand to hand, and were negotiable much as bank notes are now. But the first banker, pure and simple, was Francis Child, once the apprentice of a goldsmith, who lived frugally and decently, and pointed his career with a moral by marrying his master's richly endowed daughter.

The desirability of a national bank became apparent in many ways. It was necessary for the support of the national credit, and for the security of a paper currency. It promised to be a means of reducing the rate of interest paid by the state, and of restoring the coinage, which had become vitiated through fraud and wear, to a legitimate standard. In 1678, sixteen years previous to the foundation of the Bank of England, proposals were made for a model bank, and in 1683 a "national bank of credit" was projected. Neither of these was exactly what was wanted, and neither was carried out. The scheme upon which the Bank of England founded itself was a substantial one.

The success of the Bank of England attracted the attention of moneyed men and many were anxious to follow in its footsteps. Active competition was promised. A bank was proposed by Dr. Hugh Chamberlain, to advance money on the security of landed property. A company was formed and this wonderful project seemed to be on the eve of consummation. Unable to get money at the appointed time the scheme fell through. Many other schemes sprang up that promised to live, but faded away.

Dr. Chamberlain's scheme for a bank, as a competitor of the Bank of England, proposed to lend money at a low rate of interest on the security of land. The following is an extract from one of the doctor's proposals:—

"What we call commodities, is nothing but land severed from the soil. Man deals in nothing but earth. The merchants are the factors of the world, to exchange one part of the earth's produce for another. The King is fed by the labors of the ox; and the clothing of the army and the victualling of the navy must all be paid for to the owner of the soil, as the ultimate receiver. All things in the world are originally the produce of the ground, and thence must all things be raised."

The principal difference between this scheme of a bank and that of the Bank of England, in opposition to which corporation, then in its infancy and struggling with difficulties, this project was started, was, that no money was ever to be lent on personal security, but exclusively on title deeds of unencumbered freehold land. The bank was christened the "National Land Bank." Enough subscriptions could not be obtained within the prescribed time, consequently the scheme was a failure.

The business of banking had meanwhile been undertaken in several of the country towns of England. They met with varying success. Nearly all the banks issued their own notes, payable to bearer as part of their business; and they were not very scrupulous in regard to the magnitude of the sums for which they were given. Many of the country banks in England, still in existence, trace back their history to the latter half of the last century.

The termination of the War for Independence in America was followed in England by a great industrial and commercial development. Agriculture, commerce, and still more, manufactures, into which Watt and Arkwright's inventions had been introduced, immediately began to advance with a rapidity unknown at any former period. In consequence, that confidence which had either been destroyed, or very much weakened by the disastrous events of the war, was fully re-established. The extended transactions of the rapidly developing country required fresh facilities for carrying them on, and these were supplied to the utmost profusion. The number of banks in England, which in 1784 was certainly under 150, increased so rapidly, that in 1792 they amounted to about 350. A phenomenal increase for those days. A banking office was opened in every market town and in most villages of suitable size. Such being the case, it is needless, perhaps, to add, that the prudence, capital, character and connections of those who set up these establishments were but little looked into or attended to. The great object of a large class of traders was to obtain discounts; and the bankers of an inferior description were equally anxious to accommodate them. All sorts of papers were thus forced into circulation and enjoyed nearly the same degree of esteem. The bankers and those with whom they dealt had the fullest confidence in each other. These bankers generally lived in regal splendor, entertained handsomely and gave outward evidence of untold wealth. No one seemed to suspect that there was anything hollow or unsound in the system. Credit of every kind was strained to the utmost; and the available funds at the disposal of the bankers were reduced far below the level which the magnitude of their transactions required to render them secure. Trouble was brewing unseen on every hand.

The catastrophe which followed was such as might easily have been foreseen. The currency having become redundant, the exchanges took an unfavorable turn in the early part of 1792. A difficulty of obtaining financial accommodation in London was not long after experienced; and, notwithstanding the honest efforts of the Bank of England to mitigate the pressure, a violent revulsion took place in the latter part of 1792 and the beginning of 1793. The failure of one or two great houses excited a panic which proved fatal to many more. Out of the 350 country banks in England and Wales, when this revulsion began, about 300 were compelled to stop payments, and upwards of fifty were totally destroyed, producing by their fall an extent of misery and bankruptcy till then unknown in the country.

Attempts have at times been made to show that this crisis was not occasioned by an excess of paper money having been forced into circulation, but by the agitation caused by the war then on the eve of breaking out. Others contend that there does not seem to be any good grounds for the opinion, and cite the symptoms of an overflow of paper—a fall of the exchange, and an efflux of the exchange—which took place only in 1792, or about twelve months before the breaking out of war.

The journals of the period show that the bank had no pleasant path to pursue. The goldsmiths and private money loaners were jealous of their great competitor. Their business was diminished; their discounts were lowered; their transactions with the government had passed to the Bank of England. For years, owing to foreign funds and internal division, the directors experienced great difficulties. Nothing but strong will, unconquerable energy, and a healthy perseverance, bore them on to a triumphant issue. Looking upon the Bank of England in its present pre-eminent position, it is difficult to imagine it borne down or disturbed by jealous rivalry; struggling for a precarious existence, and laboring with an unheard of zeal to preserve itself. The bank easily triumphed over all of its enemies.

In 1708 the directors undertook to pay off and cancel one million and a half of the exchequer bills they had circulating two years before at 4½ per cent. with the interest upon them, amounting in all to £1,755,028, which increased the permanent debt due by the public to the bank, including £400,000 then advanced in consideration of the renewal of the charter, to £3,375,028, for which they were allowed 6 per cent.

The year 1708 is memorable in the history of the Bank of England for the passage by Parliament of a law which declared that during the continuance of the corporation of the Bank of England, it should not be lawful for any body politic, erected or to be erected, other than the said governor and company of the Bank of England, or of any other persons whatsoever, united or to be united in covenants or partnership, exceeding the number of six persons, in that part of Great Britain called England, to borrow, owe, or take up any sum or sums of money on their bills or notes payable on demand or in any less time than six months from the borrowing thereof. This proviso is said to have been elicited from the fact of a rival company having commenced the banking business and begun to issue notes.

It will be seen on examination of the above that the proviso did not prohibit the formation of associations for general banking business; it simply, but absolutely, forbade the issue of notes by associations of more than six partners. The issuance of notes was regarded as so essential to the business of banking that it came to be believed that joint-stock banking associations were absolutely prohibited in England, and no such association was founded until 1826, and then only after special legislation permitting them.

As previously stated, the year 1708 will be ever memorable in the history of the Bank of England and of England itself. In this year the government was led into making the Bank of England a gigantic financial monopoly, a move which wrought irretrievable ruin to many banking houses.

In consequence of this law all the joint-stock banks doing business were compelled to wind up their affairs.

The Act tacitly gave encouragement to small shopkeepers and others, however limited their means, to establish banks and issue notes; but to persons of capital, respectability and credit, willing to associate in large bodies and embark in a similar undertaking, it in fact said, "your company shall not consist of more than six partners," thereby placing the banking system in a state of liberty as to everything rotten and bad, and in a state of restriction as to everything good and substantial. Even to this day there is no part of English laws more complicated, or less understood, than the laws relating to partnership; they seem to be founded upon no general principle, and consequently are contradictory and obscure.

This state of affairs was continued until 1825, when an Act was passed allowing co-partnerships of more than six persons to carry on business in England as bankers, sixty-five miles from London, with the provision, however, that such stockholders should be liable for the entire debts of the bank. Notwithstanding the provisions of this law, which would seem to prevent any joint-stock bank being established within sixty-five miles of London, in 1834 the London and Westminister bank was founded, and has been in operation ever since, although not without having innumerable troubles to encounter. Litigation with the Bank of England, caused by a too fierce competition, and other difficulties, at first beset it, but through all of these it has passed, and met with the highest success. The success of the bank encouraged others, and in and about London are to be found plenty of them.

It must be borne in mind, however, that there are to-day (1888) no English joint-stock banks of issue except such as were formed prior to the passage of what is known as the 1844 Bank Act, which prohibited joint-stock banks from setting up within sixty-five miles of London. And these were all situated beyond the sixty-five mile limit, but as a matter of fact the privilege of issue is very little regarded in England to-day. The issuing banks have a right to issue £5,512,000—but they only have in circulation, October, 1888, £2,560,000.

The celebrated Act of 1844, which is described at length further on, affected the Bank of England in many ways. Up to this period the bank, as also private banks with not more than six partners, and since the year 1826, joint-stock banks beyond a radius of sixty-five miles from London, could issue notes without restriction, with the "promise to pay" expressed upon the notes was guaranteed only by the desire and ability of the issuers to keep faith with the holders of them. The Act of 1844 prohibited in future all issues by newly formed private or joint-stock banks, and by those which had from any cause ceased to issue prior to that date, or should do so subsequently; and restricted such issues as then existed within certain fixed amounts.

"The trade of banking," says Sir Henry Parnell, "is of such a nature, that it is scarcely possible for any but a very numerous body of partners to furnish a capital sufficiently large for carrying it on advantageously to the public. A single individual, or a few individuals, cannot be, but very rarely, possessed of that amount of capital which alone can render this trade a safe one ; for this reason, in order to establish in a country a sound system of banking, it is indispensably necessary that care should be taken not to impose any legislative restrictions in the way of large bodies associating together to form joint-stock banking companies."

CHAPTER VI.

SUSPENSION OF CASH PAYMENTS.

Important Epoch in the History of English Banking—Passage of the Restriction Act—The Government Advises with the Bank—Run on Country Banks—Bank of England Again in Trouble—Suspension of Cash Payments—Embarking on a New Course—The Bank Issues a Notice to the Public—Increase in Country Banks in 1797—Cause of Enormous Failures—Extending the Field for Circulation of Bank of England Paper—History of Depreciation of Currency—Paper Raised to Par by Accidental Circumstances.

THE year 1797 was a most important epoch in the history of English banking. Owing partly to events connected with the war then carried on, to loans to the Emperor of Germany, to bills drawn on the treasury at home by the British agents abroad, and partly, and chiefly, perhaps, to the advances most unwillingly made by the bank to the government, which prevented the directors from having a sufficient control over their issues, the exchanges became unfavorable in 1795, and in that and the following year large sums of specie were drawn from the bank. In the end of 1796 and beginning of 1797, considerable apprehensions were entertained of invasions, and rumors were propagated of descents having been actually made on the coast. In consequence of the fears that were thus excited, runs were made on the provincial banks in different parts of the country; and some of them having failed, the panic became general and extended itself to London. Demands for cash poured in from all quarters upon the bank, which, on Saturday, the 25th of February, 1797, had only £1,272,000 of cash and bullion in its coffers with every prospect of a violent run taking place on the following Monday. In this emergency, an order in council was issued on Sunday, the 26th, prohibiting the directors from paying their notes in cash until the sense of Parliament should be taken on the subject. And after Parliament met, and the measure had been much discussed, it was agreed to continue the restriction till six months after the signature of a definitive treaty of peace.

We have now come to a period in the history of banking marked by one of the most extraordinary circumstances that ever happened in England, namely, the stoppage of the issue of specie in their customary payments by the Bank of England. We are now approaching one of the most important and critical periods in the history of the bank. We propose, therefore, to give somewhat in detail a gradual development of its condition, and the real causes which led to the final suspension of all payments in cash, together with the consequences which followed that suspension.

On the 15th of January, 1795, the Court of Directors of the Bank of England passed a resolution that the Chancellor of the Exchequer be requested to make such arrangements in his finances of the present year as not to depend on any further assistance from them beyond what had already been agreed on; and on the 16th of April the governor and deputy-governor were directed to wait upon a representative of the government to express the uneasiness they felt at being called upon to pay upwards of two millions in treasury bills, and to request the government to provide for their discharge.

On the 8th of October, 1795, the Court of Directors sent a written paper to the Chancellor of the Exchequer, purporting that the very large and continued drain of bullion and specie which the bank had lately experienced, arising from loans and other subsidies, together with the prospect of the demand for gold not appearing soon to cease, had excited such apprehension in the Court of Directors that, on the most serious deliberation, they deemed it right to communicate to the Chancellor of the Exchequer the absolute necessity they conceived to exist for diminishing the sum of their present advances to the government, the last having been granted with great reluctance on their part; and then only on his pressing solicitations, and statement that serious embarrassments would arise to the public service if the bank refused.

No reply was made to this application, or any steps taken by the Chancellor of the Exchequer to relieve the bank from the difficulties in which they found themselves; but they were left to struggle through them as best they might. The directors of the bank waited on the government on the 25th of the same month, on the subject of a contemplated loan to the Emperor of Austria, and were informed that no such loan was contemplated.

Several communications appear to have passed between the bank and government from this time until the 20th of July, 1796, on which day the bank received a letter from the government requiring several advances of money including the payment of the treasury bills; and, after a debate on the subject of the letter, the court came to several resolutions, which resulted in a compliance with the government's request, with this significant addition, that such compliance be accompanied with a MOST SERIOUS AND SOLEMN RESOLUTION, which, for the justification of the court, they desire may be laid before his Majesty's cabinet. This remonstrance concluded as follows:—

"They (the Court of Directors) beg leave to declare that nothing could induce them, under present circumstances, to comply with the demand made upon them, but that the dread of their refusal might be productive of a greater evil; and nothing but the extreme pressure and exigency of the case can, in any shape, justify them for acceding to this measure, and they apprehend in so doing they render themselves totally incapable of granting any further assistance to government during the remainder of this year, and unable to make the usual advances on the land and malt taxes for the ensuing year; should those bills be passed before Christmas. They likewise consent to this measure in a firm reliance that the repeated promises so frequently made to them, that the advances on the treasury bills should be completely done away, may be actually fulfilled at the next meeting of Parliament, and the necessary arrangements taken to prevent the same from ever happening again, as they conceive it to be an unconstitutional mode of raising money; what they are not warranted by their charter to consent to; and an advance always extremely inconvenient to themselves."

By this confession on the part of the bank, it appears that they were in the habit of violating that clause in their charter which prohibits their lending any money to the King without the consent of Parliament.

On the 9th of February, 1797, the Court of Directors ordered the governor of the bank to notify the government that, under the present state of the bank's advances to government, to agree to his request of making a further advance of £1,500,000 as a loan to Ireland, would threaten ruin to the bank, and most probably bring the directors under the necessity of shutting up their doors.

These several remonstrances to the government seem to have had little or no effect; and the result anticipated, viz.: a stoppage of the Bank of England, took place even at an earlier period than the directors themselves calculated upon.

The run—to speak in commercial phraseology—commenced upon some of the country bankers; and the great demand for specie to supply them induced the directors to lay the state of their affairs before the government.

His Majesty's Privy Council held a meeting and the following resulted:

"Upon the representation of the Chancellor of the Exchequer, stating, that from the result of the information he has received, and of the inquiries which it has been his duty to make respecting the effect of the unusual demand for specie that has been made upon the metropolis, in consequence of ill-founded alarms in different parts of the country ; it appears, that unless some measure is immediately taken, there may be reason to apprehend a want of a sufficient supply of cash to answer the exigencies of the public service. It is the unanimous opinion of the Board, that it is indispensably necessary for the public service that the directors of the Bank of England should forbear issuing any cash in payment until the sense of Parliament can be taken on that subject, and the proper measures adopted thereupon for maintaining the means of circulation, and supporting the public and commercial credit of the Kingdom at this important juncture. And it ordered that a copy of this minute be transmitted to the directors of the Bank of England at once."

On the next Monday morning the following was issued by the bank:—

"In consequence of an order of his Majesty's Privy Council, notified to the bank last night, the Governor, Deputy Governor, and Directors of the Bank of England think it is their duty to inform the proprietors of the bank stock, as well as the public at large, that the general concerns of the bank are in the most affluent and flourishing condition, and such as to preclude every doubt as to the security of its notes. The Directors mean to continue their usual discounts, for the accommodation of the commercial interests, paying the amount in bank notes; and the dividend warrants will be paid in the same manner."

Great alarm was excited throughout London on the appearance of the above notice.

By the order of the Privy Council the Directors of the Bank of England were restrained from doing what in fact was physically impossible for them to do; and were indulged with the liberty of exchanging one promise to pay for another promise to pay, yet, notwithstanding this suspension of cash payments, which forms a most memorable era in the history of political economy, the credit of the bank immediately revived, and their notes were circulated more freely than ever, and retained the same degree of credit as when, according to the tenor of their promises, they were honored with an immediate payment.

The bank was determined to act up to the letter and spirit of the order of the Privy Council; for they even refused to furnish the bankers of the metropolis with a sufficient quantity of specie to pay the fractional part of the checks drawn on them; and in reply to the application of the Committee of Bankers, stated:—"They could not spare the specie."

The moment the Bank of England on authority refused to pay their notes, the legislature without doubt became responsible for the validity of that currency which they had hitherto only connived at.

As previously stated, as soon as the order in council prohibiting payments in cash appeared, a meeting of the principal bankers, merchants, traders, &c., of the metropolis, was held, when a resolution was agreed to, and very numerously signed, pledging those present to accept, and to use every means in their power to make bank-notes be accepted, as cash in all transactions. This resolution tended to allay the apprehensions that the restriction had excited.

Parliament being in session at the time, a committee was immediately appointed to examine into the affairs of the bank; and their report put to rest whatever doubts might have been entertained with respect to the solvency of the establishment, by showing, that at the moment when the order in council appeared, the bank was possessed of property to the amount of £15,513,690, after all claims upon it had been deducted. This suspension of cash payments being naturally followed by a withdrawal of gold from circulation, made it necessary to allow of the issue of notes of a smaller denomination than £5, and the statute of 1777 was accordingly also suspended.

It had been generally supposed, previously to the passing of the Restriction Act, that bank-notes would not circulate unless they were immediately convertible into cash. But the event showed that this was not really the case. Though the notes of the Bank of England were not, at the passing of the Restriction Act, declared by law to be legal tender, they were rendered such in practice, by being received as cash in all payments on account of government, and by the vast majority of individuals. For the first three years of the restriction, their issues were so moderate that they not only kept on a par with gold, but actually bore a small premium. But in 1801, 1802, and 1803, they were so much increased that they fell to a discount of from 8 to 10 per cent. In 1804 they again recovered their value; and from that year to 1808, both inclusive, they were at a discount of 2½ per cent. In 1809 and 1810, however, the directors appear to have embarked on a new course, and to have entirely lost sight of the principles by which their issues had previously been governed;

for the average amount of bank-notes in circulation, which had not exceeded 17½ millions, nor fallen short of 16½ millions, in any one year, from 1802 to 1808, both inclusive, was in 1809 raised to £18,927,833, and 1810 to £22,541,523. The issues of country bank paper were increased in a still greater proportion; and, as there was no corresponding increase of the business of the country, the discount on bank-notes rose from 2½ in 1808 to from 13 to 16 per cent. in 1809 and 1810.

This depreciation in the value of bank paper being accompanied by a corresponding fall in the exchange, attracted the attention of the public and the legislature. In consequence, the House of Commons appointed, in 1810, a committee to inquire into the subject; and having examined several witnesses, the committee in their report, which was both an able and a celebrated paper, justly ascribed the fall in the value of bank paper, as compared with gold, to its over-issue; and recommended, in the view of correcting the existing evil and of preventing its recurrence, that within two years the bank should be obliged to resume specie payments. But this recommendation not being adopted, the over-issue of paper went on increasing. In 1812 it was at an average discount, as compared with bullion, of 20 per cent.; in 1813, of 23 per cent.; and in 1814, when the maximum of depreciation was attained, it was at 25 per cent.

At the period when the restriction on cash payments took place in 1797, it is supposed that there were about 280 country banks in existence; but so rapidly were these establishments multiplied, that they amounted to above 900 in 1813. The price of corn, influenced partly by the depreciation of the currency and the facility with which discounts were obtained, but more by deficient harvests and the unprecedented difficulties which the war threw in the way of importation, rose to an extraordinary height during the five years ending with 1813. But the harvest of that year being unusually productive, and the intercourse with the Continent being then also renewed, prices, influenced by both circumstances, sustained a very heavy fall in the latter part of 1813 and the beginning of 1814. And this fall having ruined a considerable number of farmers and produced a general want of confidence, such a destruction of provincial paper took place as has rarely been paralleled. In 1814, 1815, and 1816, no fewer than 240 country banks stopped payment; and *eighty-nine* commissions of bankruptcy were issued against these establishments, being at the rate of *one* commission against every *ten and a half* of the total number of banks existing in 1813.

The great reduction that was thus suddenly and violently brought about in the quantity of country bank paper, by extending the field for the circulation of Bank of England paper, raised its value in 1817 nearly to a par with gold. The return to cash payments being thus facilitated, it was fixed, in 1819, that they should take place in 1823. But to prevent any future over issue, and at the same time to render the resumption as little burdensome as possible, it was enacted that the banks should be obliged, during the interval from the passing of the Act till the return to specie payments, to pay its notes, if required, in bars of standard bullion of not less than sixty ounces' weight. This plan was not, however, acted upon during the period allowed by law ; for, a large amount of gold having been accumulated at the bank, the directors preferred recommencing specie payments on the 1st of May, 1821.

It is true, that after a currency has been for a considerable period depreciated, as much injustice is done by raising, as was previously done by depressing, its value. But there is good reason to doubt whether the depreciation from 1809 to 1815 (for the depreciation of 2½ per cent. during the six preceding years is too inconsiderable to be taken into account) extended over a sufficiently lengthened period to warrant legislation looking for a departure from the old standard. It is needless, however, to offer any opinion on this rather difficult point, for we have seen that the value of paper was raised in 1816 and 1817 almost to par by accidental circumstances without any interference on the part of the government or the bank. Sir Robert Peel's Act, to which this raise has been ascribed, not being passed till 1819, could have nothing to do with what occurred two or three years previously. Its object was two-fold, to redeem the pledge given by Parliament to restore the old standard on the return of peace, and to shut the door against any further depreciation of paper.

CHAPTER VII.

SPECULATIONS, SCHEMES, FAILURES AND LOSSES.

Bank of England Resumes Cash Payments—Vicissitudes of Banking—Speculative Rage—No Scheme Too Hazardous—Speculation of To-Day Not Without a Precedent—Worthless Paper Readily Negotiated—Discounts Easily Obtained—Schemes of Country Bankers—A Cyclone of Failures—Bank of England Makes a Serious Blunder—Distrust Fully Awake—A Tremendous Run—Cause of the Difficulties—An Instructive Table—Accumulation of Securities—What the Directors Should Have Done to Avoid Disaster—Loss of Three Millions of Bullion—The South Sea Bubble—A Delirium of Speculation—List of the Bubble Companies of 1721—Getting Rich Without Trouble—Philanthropist Thomas Guy.

THE resumption of cash payments did not, however, put an end to the vicissitudes of banking. Notwithstanding the ample experience that had been supplied by the occurrences of 1792-3, and 1814-16, of the mischievous consequences of the issue of paper by the country banks, and of their want of solidity, nothing whatever was done when provision was made for returning to specie payment to restrain their issues, or to place them on a better footing. The consequences of such improvidence were not long in manifesting themselves. The price of corn and other agricultural products, which had been greatly depressed in consequence of abundant harvests, in 1820, 1821, and 1822, rallied in 1823, and the country bankers immediately began to enlarge their issues. It is hardly necessary to look into the circumstances which conspired, along with the rise of prices, to promote the extraordinary rage for speculation exhibited in 1824 and 1825. It is sufficient to observe, that in consequence of their operation, confidence was very soon carried to the greatest height. It did not seem to be supposed that any scheme could be hazardous, much less wild or extravagant. Wild American speculation, occasionally seen, is tame compared with the wild business ventures and speculations in England in the years named above. So speculation, after all, as seen to-day, is not without its precedent.

In those days the infatuation for speculation was such, that even those regarded as the most conservative and considerate did not scruple to embark in visionary and the most utterly absurd projects; while the extreme facility with which discounts were procured upon bills at very long dates, afforded the means of carrying on every sort of undertaking. The most worthless paper was readily negotiated. Many of the country bankers seemed to have no other object than to get themselves indebted to the public. And such was the vigor and success of their efforts to force their paper into circulation, that the amount of it afloat in 1825 is estimated to have been nearly 60 per cent. greater than in 1823. The consequence of this unprincipled and extravagant conduct speedily brought ruin to all engaged.

Now came a cyclone of failures, the direct outgrowth of speculation, the like of which was never experienced before, seventy banks going under in six weeks, the majority, of course, being country banks. The currency having become redundant, the exchange began to decline in the summer of 1824. The directors of the Bank of England having unwarily entered, in the early part of that year, into an engagement with the government to pay off such holders of 4 per cent. stock as might dissent from its conversion into a 3½ per cent. stock, were obliged to advance a considerable sum on this account after the depression of the exchange. But despite this circumstance, they might and ought to have taken measures, in the latter part of 1824 and the earlier part of 1825, by lessening their issues to stop the efflux of bullion. But not being sufficiently alive to the urgency of the crisis, the London currency was not materially diminished till September, 1825. The recoil, which would have been less severe had the efforts of the bank to prevent the exhaustion of its coffers taken place at an earlier period, was most appalling.

The country banks began to give way the moment they experienced a considerably increased difficulty of obtaining accommodation in London, and confidence and credit were immediately at an end. Suspicion having awakened from her trance, distrust had no limits. All classes of depositors made haste to draw out the money they had entrusted to the care of the banks. There was also a tremendous run upon them for payment of their notes, not in the view of sending the gold as a mercantile adventure to the Continent, but to escape the loss which it became obvious the holders of country paper would have to sustain. *Sauve qui peut* was the universal cry; and the destruction was so sudden and extensive, that in less than six weeks more than seventy banking establishments were swept out of existence, and a vacuum was created in the currency which absorbed from eight to ten millions of additional issues by the Bank of England at the same time that myraids of those private bills that had previously swelled the amount of currency, and added to the machinery of speculation, were totally destroyed.

It may be worth while, perhaps, to observe that it has been alleged, in opposition to what is now stated, that the difficulties of the bank in 1825 were not caused by any excess either of its issues as of those of the country banks, but by the too great amount of capital, that is of coin and bullion, it had lent; and in proof of this allegation, we are referred to the increase of nearly eight millions in securities which the bank held in August, 1825, over their amount in August, 1822, and to the simultaneous decrease of nearly six and a half millions in the amount of bullion in its coffers. The following statement is instructive:—

Securities of all sorts, 31st August, 1822,.... £17,290,510
" " 31st August, 1825,.... 25,106,030
Excess of securities, 31st August, 1825, over those held on 31st August, 1822,...... £7,815,520

Bullion in Bank, 31st August, 1822,......... £10,097,960
"   "   31st August, 1825,......... 3,634,320
           Diminution of bullion,......... £6,463,640

On the 28th February, 1826, the bullion in the bank amounted to only £2,459,510.

A little consideration will suffice to show the futility of this statement. No issue of notes can be said to be in itself excessive. Whether it is or is not in excess depends upon its relation to the amount of coin and bullion reserved by the issuing banks in its coffers. The Bank of England enlarged its issues disproportionately and took no steps, or none of sufficient energy, to reduce the amount of notes in circulation till long after the exchange had become unfavorable, and bullion was demanded of it for exportation.

The accumulation of securities was the necessary result of this radical error. The currency having become redundant in 1824, the notes of the bank were returned upon it for gold, so that its securities were augmented at the same time that its means of dealing with the unfavorable exchange were impaired. It should be remembered, that the efflux of bullion showed conclusively that, however issued, and whether greater or less than at former periods, the paper afloat was in excess, and that its reduction had become indispensable. And such being the case, it was the duty of the bank directors, as soon as they felt the drain for gold setting steadily against them, to adopt every means in their power, by raising the rate of interest, selling securities, and otherwise, to reduce their issues and restore the exchange to par. And had they done this at a sufficiently early period, it is all but certain the bank would not have lost more than two or three millions of bullion; whereas, by their following a different line of conduct, and deferring the adoption of vigorous repressive measures till too late a period, it was drained of about seven millions of bullion, and its safety seriously compromised before it could stop the drain.

The speculative rage before mentioned was not without precedent. The South Sea Company was the leader of the maddest kind of schemes and speculations England, or in fact any other country, ever saw. The memorable project for the formation of the South Sea Company was brought out in the year 1711, and owed its origin to the following circumstances :—

During the war with France, in the reign of King William the Third, the payments to the sailors of the English navy being neglected, they received tickets instead of money, and they were frequently obliged, by their necessities, to sell their tickets at forty, and sometimes fifty, per cent. below the amount for which they received them. By this and other means the debts of the nation unprovided for by Parliament, amounted together to £9,471,325. Mr. Harley, at that time Chancellor of the Exchequer, proposed a scheme to allow the holders of these tickets or debentures, and the other portion of the floating debt, six per cent. per annum interest, and to incorporate them for the purpose of carrying on a trade to the South Seas; and they were accordingly incorporated under the title of the Governor and Company of merchants of Great Britain, trading to the South Seas and other parts of America, and for encouraging the Fisheries.

The company soon abandoned all idea of mercantile

operations—if they ever seriously intended to undertake them—and confined themselves to money dealings with the government, and increasing the value of their stock, which at one time rose to the enormous amount of 1,000 per cent.

The apparent success of the South Sea Company scheme caused numerous romantic projects, proposals and undertakings, both private and national, to be submitted to the public, many of which were notoriously absurd. Persons of rank of both sexes were deeply engaged in these bubbles; avarice prevailing at this time over all consideration, either of dignity or equity, the gentlemen going to taverns and coffee-houses to meet their brokers, and the ladies to their milliners' and haberdashers' shops for the like purpose.

Any impudent imposter, while the speculative delirium was at its height, needed only to hire a room at some coffee-house, or other resort, near the exchange, for a few hours, and open a subscription book for something relative to commerce, manufactures, plantations, or some supposed invention, newly hatched out of his own brain. These delusive projects, a list of some of the most ridiculous of which will be found below, received their first check from the power to which they owed their birth, viz.: the South Sea Company, the directors of which, desirious to monopolize all the money of the speculators to themselves, obtained writs of *scire facias* against the conductors of the bubbles.

A LIST OF THE BUBBLES, AS PUBLISHED IN THE YEAR 1721.

Hard Soap.

Potato Starch.

Silver Extract.
Men's Breeches.
Fattening Hogs.
South Sea Hops.
Swords from Iron.
Bleaching of Hair.
Butter Manufactory.
Overall's Fire Office.
Employing the Poor.
Fishery for Gudgeons.
Suppression of Piracy.
Improvements of Hops.
Women's Silk Stockings.
Ladies' Hoop Petticoats.
Trade to the North Seas.
Grand American Fishery.
Grand Fishery for Smelts.
Improvements in Tobacco.
Exportation of Old Clothes.
Insurance Against Burglars.
Hurst's Importation of Hair.
Insuring Children's Fortunes.
Insurance Against Highwaymen.
A New Method for Cleaning Streets.
Serving London with Hay and Corn.
Curing of Broken Winded Horses and Mares.
Melting Sawdust and Shavings into Deal Boards of any length and free from knots.

The bursting of these bubbles left traces of misery and distress to an extent hitherto unknown in the monetary world.

The credulity of the British public at this period was only surpassed by the impudence of the inventor. Men, without any capital but presumption, proposed and carried out companies; and when, by the aid of an important name or two, obtained, perhaps, under fraudulent pretences, and a prospectus full of specious phraseology and definite promises, they had arrived at a premium, the shares were sold and the associations abandoned.

In a satirical novel of the day, a bubble company to be called "The Gold, Wine and Olive Joint-Stock Company," is supposed to be projected. From the writer's position, it is very probable that much of his presumed fiction was facts. "All we have to do," says one of the projectors, "is to puff our shares up to a premium, humbug the public into buying them, and then let the whole concern go to ruin." There was also presented for public favor the prospectus of a company to drain the Red Sea, in search of the gold and jewels left by the Egyptians, in their passage after the Israelites. Many similar jocculosities were in circulation, some of which emanated from the members of the Stock Exchange, always alive to a sense of the ridiculous. But it is impossible, and the experience of every speculative era has proved it, to open the eyes of men who are making large profits. Every one appeared to get rich without trouble. The price of all articles increased in value. Ten-fold higher terms were paid for land, with the view of building on it, than it was worth.

"The wildness of speculation," says Knight's History of London, "was not, however, confined to joint-stock projects; but at length reached to commercial produce generally. Money was abundant, and circulated with rapidity. Prices and profits rose higher and higher, and, in short,

> 'All went merry as a marriage bell.'"

The newspapers and periodicals of the day could scarcely contain the announcements which day after day poured from the prolific pens of schemers. Shares were issued at high premiums; loan after loan was taken at high rates; but high as they were contracted, the extravagant feeling of the period sent them all higher. The shopkeeper ceased to toil, that he might become suddenly rich. The merchant embarked his capital and his credit; the clerk risked his reputation and his place, to obtain a share of the broad golden stream, which waited to be drunk. The broker could scarcely find time to execute his commissions. There was one individual who looked calmly on during the progress of these schemes and bubbles, and although not profiting at the expense of the credulity of the people engaged in them, had reaped an immense fortune by foreseeing at their commencement the events that actually occurred. That individual was Thomas Guy, the founder of Guy's Hospital. Mr. Guy was a bookseller.

We have before stated that such was the poverty of the Exchequer at the latter part of the reign of King William the Third, money could not be obtained for paying the seamen's wages, and that they were accordingly paid by tickets or debentures, which, from their necessities, they were compelled to part with considerably below their nominal value. The purchasers of these tickets were in turn obliged to sell them; and at one time such was their depreciation that they fell to fifty per cent. discount.

Mr. Guy, having been a thrifty, saving man, had realized what in those days was considered a large sum of money; and, having the utmost possible confidence in the honor and integrity of the government, that the debentures would one day—and that at no distant period—be paid in full, was one of the first to set an example of investing his capital in government securities, by purchasing a considerable quantity of this "floating debt," as it was then called. The result was that out of his investments he eventually realized several million pounds.

The cost of erecting Guy's Hospital was £18,793, and of endowing it £219,499, together £238,292, which munificent gift, during his lifetime, was a much larger sum than had ever before been dedicated by a single individual to charitable purposes. It even rivalled the endowment of Kings. Thomas Guy died December 27, 1724, in the eightieth year of his age. Sixteen years before his death he built and furnished the wards in St. Thomas's Hospital, for the reception of sixty-four patients. He also left to the managers of Christ's Hospital a perpetual annuity of £400 a year for taking in four children annually. He also left £1,000 to be appropriated in relieving from prison those prisoners whose debts did not exceed £5 each, by which bequest six hundred obtained their liberty. He also provided liberally for his relatives.

Although the above account does not, strictly speaking, fall within the range of subjects marked out for this work, we could not refrain from referring to a character so truly estimable and charitable as that of Thomas Guy, whose beneficence is still dispensed with the same generous sympathy for the afflicted as it was upwards of one hundred and sixty years ago.

CHAPTER VIII.

LOOSE BANKING METHODS PARALYZE BUSINESS.

Improving Country Banking—Suppressing £1 Notes— Repealing Laws—Circulation of Notes for Less than £5 Forbidden — Speculative Schemes Again in Abundance—Rage for Establishing New Banks—Voluminous Issue of Notes--Raising the Rate of Interest—Shock to Industrial Undertakings—How the Bank of England Escaped Failure—Natural Obstacle to Formation of New Banks—The Railway Mania--Gigantic Frauds Perpetrated by Projectors of Imaginary Railroads—The Country Wild with Speculation—The Crash Wrecks Thousands—A Banker's Duty—The Penalty of Neglect.

NOTWITHSTANDING the fact that nations are slow and reluctant learners, the events of 1825-26, taken in connection with those of the same sort that had previously occurred, produced a conviction of the necessity of doing something that should at least improve the system of country banking in England. But the measures adopted with this view were very far indeed from effectually securing their object. The law of 1708, limiting to six the number of partners in banking establishments issuing notes, was repealed; and it was enacted, that banks with any number of partners might be established for the issue of notes anywhere beyond sixty-five miles from London, and that banks not issuing notes might be established in London itself with any number of partners. The circulation of notes for less than five pounds in England and Wales was at the same time forbidden. It was intended to extend the same prohibition to Scotland and Ireland, but the opposition to the proposal excited in these countries was too strong to be overcome. Sir Walter Scott threw himself zealously into the controversy, and by his *Letters of Malachi Malagrowther*, helped to make the resistance effectual.

The suppression of £1 notes was advantageous in shutting up one of the principal channels by which the inferior class of country bankers got their paper into circulation, to the frequent loss of the poorer classes; but it is now generally admitted that the balance of argument is in favor of the issue of notes of this denomination by the Bank of England or some agency of the state, under conditions ensuring their convertibility.

The second branch of the banking legislation of 1826 was for some time a comparative failure. Those who supposed that joint-stock banks would be immediately set on foot in all parts of England, were a good deal disappointed with the slowness with which they spread for some years after the Act permitting their establishment was passed. The heavy losses occasioned by the downfall of most of the joint stock projects set on foot in 1824 and 1825, made all projects of the same kind be looked upon for a considerable period with suspicion, and deterred most persons from embarking in them. But this caution gradually wore off; and the increasing prosperity of the country, and the difficulty of investing money so to obtain from it reasonable return, generated anew a disposition to adventure in hazardous projects. A mania for embarking in speculative schemes acquired considerable strength in 1834; and during 1835 and part of 1836, it raged with a violence but little inferior to that of 1825, which is described in a previous chapter. It was at first principally directed to railroad projects; but it soon began to embrace all sorts of schemes, and, among others, joint-stock banks, of which an unprecedented number were projected in 1835. The progress of the system was as follows:—

	Banks.
In 1826 there were registered	6
In 1827	1
In 1828	5
In 1829	4
In 1830	3
In 1831	8
In 1832	10
In 1833	13
In 1834	8
In 1835	45
In 1836	11
Total	114

In point of fact, however, the number of banks created in 1835 and 1836 was vastly greater than appears from this statement. It seems that, at an average, each of the 56 banks established in those years, like those previously established, had from four to five branches; and as these branches transacted all sorts of banking business, and enjoyed the same credit as the parent establishment, from which they were frequently at a great distance, they were, to all intents and purposes, so many new banks; so that, instead of 56, it may safely be affirmed that from about 220 to 280 new joint-stock banks were opened in England and Wales in 1835 and 1836, but mostly in the former year.

In January, February, and March, 1836, when the rage for establishing joint-stock banks was at its height, the exchange was either at par, or nearly so, showing that the currency was already up to its level, and that if any considerable additions were made to it, the exchange would be depressed, and a drain for bullion be experienced. But these circumstances, if ever they occurred to the managers of the joint-stock banks, do not seem to have had, and could not in truth be expected to have, any material influence over their proceedings. Their issues, which amounted on the 26th of December, 1835 to £2,799,551, amounted on the 25th of June, 1836, to £3,588,064, exclusive of the vast mass of additional bills, checks, and other substitutes for money they had put into circulation. The consequences were such as every man of sense might have foreseen. In April, 1836, the exchange became unfavorable, and bullion began to be demanded from the Bank of England. The directors, that they might the better meet the drain, raised the rate of interest in June from 4 to 4½ per cent., and this not being enough to sufficiently lessen the pressure on the bank for discounts, they raised it in August from 4½ to 5 per cent. But during the whole of this period the country banks went on increasing their issues; and the issues of the joint-stock banks rose from £3,588,064 in June, to no less than £4,258,197 on the 31st of December, being an increase of nearly 20 per cent. after the exchange was notoriously against the country; and the most serious consequences were apprehended from the continued drain for bullion.

It may, perhaps, be supposed that the increased issue of the joint-stock banks would be balanced by a corresponding diminution of the issue of the private banks, and that on the whole the amount of their joint issues might not be increased. This, however, was not the case. Some private banks were abandoned in 1836, and others incorporated with joint-stock banks ; and it is further true, that those which went on managed their affairs with more discretion than their associated competitors. But, from the 26th of September, 1835, to the 31st of December, 1836, the issues of the private banks were diminished only £159,087, whilst those of the joint-stocks were increased during the same period £1,750,160, or more than *ten times* the falling off in the others.

These statements show the inexpediency of leaving the issue of paper to the unregulated discretion of an indefinite number of competing banks. Its issue ought in all cases to be governed by the state of the exchange, or rather, as already stated, by the influx and efflux of bullion. But previously to 1844, the provincial banks might go on over-issuing for a lengthened period without being affected by a demand for bullion, or even for Bank of England paper. In the end, no doubt, an afflux of the former was sure, by rendering money and all sorts of pecuniary accommodation scarce in the metropolis, to affect the country banks as well as the Bank of England; and then the injury to industry, occasioned by the withdrawal of their accustomed accommodations from a great number of individuals, was severe in proportion to the too great liberality with which they had previously been supplied. This was especially the case in 1836, when the Bank of England, by bolstering up neighboring banks averted a panic that would have proved fatal to nearly every joint-stock and private bank in England.

Still, the shock given to industrial undertakings, by the revulsion in the latter part of the year, and in 1837, although unaccompanied by any panic, was very severe and wide-spread. All sorts of commercial speculations were for a while completely paralyzed, and there were but few districts in which the manufacturing establishments were not closed, and thousands upon thousands thrown out of employment. In Paisley, Birmingham, Manchester, Leeds and Sheffield the distress occasioned was something terrible and long continued. And owing to the Bank of England having delayed, in 1838 and the earlier part of 1839, to take efficient measures for the reduction of its issues, despite the unmistakable evidence of their being redundant, the bullion in its coffers was reduced in September, 1839, to £2,406,000; and, but for the efficient assistance obtained from the Bank of France, its stoppage could hardly have been averted.

It might be added that with the exception of London, and some of the larger provincial towns, there have been very few banks established in England since 1836, eight years before the important Bank Charter Act of 1844, which we treat at length in the following pages, and of the banks established in 1835 and 1836, very many were formed by the conversion of pre-existing private banks into joint-stock associations. The truth appears to be that the natural obstacles to the establishment of a new bank in a district already occupied by banks and bankers are almost insuperable. A bank cannot be successful unless it commands credit; and those who want a place of safe keeping for their money select establishments that have been tried and tested through long years. Hence, it happens that, though private banks of long standing continue in esteem, the attempts to set up new private banks are most rare; and, unless the wealth and prosperity of a neighborhood have rapidly developed, so that capitalists have risen to prominence in it who are not connected as shareholders or directors with existing banks, it is not easy to form joint-stock associations of weight enough to compete with the institutions in possession of the field.

The history of the railway mania in England in 1845 is not the least remarkable among those delusions which from time to time arise to throw aside legitimate trade, and paralyze national commerce. In 1842 discounts were easy and money plentiful. The funds maintained a high rate; and low interest only could be obtained. In 1844 it was remarked that there had been a longer continuance of a plentiful supply of money than had occurred in the memory of the oldest capitalist. A desire to speculate grew out of these circumstances. Unlike most periods, when this desire has been spread over many objects, it was concentrated on railways and railway schemes; and England was again seized with her ancient frenzy that wrought so much havoc in 1825. For some time it was legitimate, and confined within its proper boundary—but the desire spread—the contagion passed to all, and from the clerk to the capitalist the speculative fever reigned, uncontrollable and uncontrolled. Some portion of the press aided the mania. The subject was a capable one, and leading articles trumpeted the growing greatness of the train.

The directors of the railways were formed of all classes, and of all conditions. Long lists of provisional committeemen, with their residences and professions, were paraded in the newspapers. The journals were in many instances increased in size to contain the numerous advertisements. Men who had mingled in the bubbles and schemes of 1825; men who were known and recognized as adventurous swindlers, but who had disappeared when no money was to be obtained, reappeared to exercise their customary vocation. Royalty partook of the excitement. Grave and sober men dabbled in scrip. The literary man and the artist risked their hard-earned money to procure a share in the profits. The youth of the empire sought to gratify expensive habits. The old man sought to indulge his avarice. The clergyman traded in "undeniable securities." The physician murmured of the broad and narrow-guage. The lawyer forsook his fee; the lady jeopardized her soft and gentle influence; the matron forgot her children, and the maiden her embroidery, in one universal pursuit. The names of the clergy on the lists of directors produced an opinion from the Bishop of Exeter, that for a clergyman to speculate in railways came under the denomination of "dealing for gain or profit," and this was against the statute. "As the statute only mentions dealing," remarked a journal of the time, "and railway speculation involves shuffling, some of the reverend gentlemen maintain that they do not violate the Act of Parliament."

The following from a periodical of the day, is undoubtedly a faithful picture of the way in which many railways were established:—

"A young gentleman need only look to a half-crown railway map, and search for a district tolerably clear of the rail. Taking two of the towns that form that open space, he draws a diagonal with his pencil, and thus creates a direct line. He then writes down the name of the company, his own name as 'promoter,' either alone, or with the names of as many friends as he can venture to take that liberty with, or with any names, real or fictitious; his own occupation, whether gentleman or esquire, engineer, artist, merchant, lawyer, clerk or tailor ; his place of business if he has one. In his walks about town he may remodel his company, changing every name in it, whether of place or person, including himself. Arriving at his office, he invests a few sovereigns, begged, borrowed, or stolen, in fees, and enters his company. Advertisements and letters of allotment do the rest. It may, for anything the registrar knows or cares, be straight across a mountain, a mile high, or straight across the arm of a sea, ten miles broad. It would be his duty to register a tunnel under the Atlantic ; and we are not quite sure that he would have the option of refusing a railroad to the moon, with extension to the planets, and a short branch to the sun."

The prospectus was sure to promise all the advantages of all the world, perhaps to some small village which had hitherto been unable to support a coach once a week. The name of a local person of influence was obtained; a meeting was called at the village inn; speeches were uttered, which discoursed most eloquent music in the ears of the villagers, for their property was to be improved, and their importance doubled. Propositions were unanimously carried with a wild huzza that a railway was necessary; the speeches appeared in the local journals with flaming head lines and were prominently advertised in London newspapers; ten times the number of shares were applied for which were issued; and when they arrived at a premium, the promoters, secretaries, and directors seized the golden opportunity, and as usual, the dear public came off second best. The socializing influences of the railway were descanted upon. Directors dreamed of premiums, patronage and pay. "Men who were known to have been penniless," writes a keen observer of that day, "suddenly kept their liveried servants and broughams, valuable diamonds gleamed from their fingers which had hitherto been guiltless of the bright adornment. Railway papers and railway pantaloons, railway ties and railway tricks, abounded. It was a railway madness. London was to be tunnelled. The names of men well known in London as swindlers whose notorious character had banished them from the society of all good men, suddenly reappeared on the lists of the proprietors and directors, their names graced by the cheap esquire, and their residences given in some far distant country."

Everyone talked of making large fortunes, and very few realized them. The same person was director of thirty different railways, under various descriptions. The crash finally came. Twelve "leading men" in the city brought out a project for a railway. The deposit was trifling, but their standing enabled them to demand a heavy premium. They cleared by this £25,000 each, and shortly afterwards sent round a circular, stating that unforeseen engineering difficulties rendered the abandonment of the scheme necessary, and, with a trifling per centage deducted for expenses, the deposits, not the premiums, were returned. An endeavor at the time to establish the truth of this produced the reply: "It is likely to be true of so many that it will be useless to fix it upon any particular company." The panic continued. The reckless speculation produced its natural results. The evil commenced to abate. The fluctuations in the periodical returns of the Bank of England were eagerly watched; and each week the apparent impossibility of paying up the deposits was confirmed. It was what has been finely termed "the rushing mania of a nation."

Of this prevailing madness, however, the evil effects remained long after the hope had departed. Many men of character, who had worked hard for the independence they had gained, had consented in an evil hour to join the committees of projected companies; in the height of their delusion they talked of large profits, made extensive purchases, and lived in a costly style; but they soon found out that they were liable for their individual risk, and many were compelled to sell their property at a sacrifice and fly to a foreign soil, from their relentless creditors. In one instance, a person who had stepped out of his legitimate path to speculate in these securities, was paying 200 per cent. in the stock Exchange at the very time that his bills were being taken at 3½ per cent. in the discount market. Railway shares and stocks suddenly became worthless. The wild speculative excitement ended. It was another proof of the fact that no warning can save a people determined to grow suddenly rich. The small trader who had neglected his calling was ruined. The merchant who had embarked in the adventurous speculations found to his cost that the reckoning was yet to come. The deposits were to be met, and many possessed no money wherewith to pay them. They had embarked in engagements which they could not fulfill, and a fearful prospect awaited them. 'Everyone who invested suffered; a few audacious scoundrels became wealthy; and a period of depression followed that has never been equaled. Through this memorable crisis the Bank of England played an important though successful part.

Bankers possess, from their peculiar position, very superior means of distinguishing the careful from the improvident trader; indeed, it is considered as a regular branch of their professional experience, that they should appreciate the credit of the various traders within the district which their business transactions are supposed to cover. It is becoming now the practice of bankers to communicate, confidentially, with each other, touching the credit of individuals and firms within their bailiwicks.

A banker, in his character as trustee for others, should be at all times a man of decision, and have a general knowledge of the respectability and responsibility of the mercantile community, especially of his own neighborhood. The science of banking is not intuitive; there is no golden road to it. A man may be rich and powerful in his neighborhood, and looked up to as a man of wealth; but, as the taking care of his own estate is not banking, his character as a banker only commences when he has to take care of, and judiciously employ, the moneys of other people entrusted to him.

It is by neglecting to watch narrowly the operations of commercial men, that bankers are too often instrumental in causing, not only the failure of their customers, but of themselves also. To avoid as much as possible this state of things, a banker should, at the proper time, be able to negative the applications made to him for assistance, and on no account to allow feelings of personal nature to get the better of his judgment.

Most bankers in the country carry on their business of borrowing or receiving money at interest, as well as lending upon securities, and they thereby form a connecting link in the chain between the operative and unoperative classes; they become the debtors of the capitalists and the creditors of the producers or distributors of revenue, and thus afford a ready medium of adjustment between the interests of these two great divisions of society. It is therefore the chief object of his study, and his constant desire to search out and to make choice of the most secure, as well as the most profitable employment of the capital which is thus placed under his charge, and for the safety of which he is held responsible.

CHAPTER IX.

BANK OF ENGLAND HANDLED BY PARLIAMENT.

The Famous 1844 Bank Act—Sir Robert Peel Battling for Reform—Providing a Remedy for Instability—Financial Writers Interested—Peel's Speech on the Renewal of the Bank's Charter—Important Provisions of the New Law—Price Paid for Exclusive Privilege of Banking—Suspending the Bank Act in 1866—Fundamental Principle upon which English Currency Rests—The Law and the Bank—The Bank's Control of Its Capital.

THE position of the country in 1844 was indeed critical. A feeling of discontent was prevalent among the agrarian and manufacturing population. An empty treasury, a failing revenue, and a dissatisfied people, were sufficient to render the government of the nation a difficult task. The labors of the officers of the bank were greatly increased by the deduction of the property tax from more than half a million of dividends belonging to the public creditor, and the interests of the bank were yet more deeply involved in this tax, as it opened the question with regard to the justice of paying the charges upon terminable annuities. In many instances these annuities would expire in a very few years; and in the case of the bank, which possessed the dead weight and other annuities, entered into without any idea of such a tax, it appeared to the proprietors a very objectionable impost. It was argued by these gentlemen that it would not be equitable to compel them to pay the income tax on annuities, as it would be in reality paying on the capital. It was resolved to memorialize the government on the question, but the attempt was vain, and it was determined that no difference should be made between the dividend of the bond-holder and the payment of the annuitant.

The advent of Sir Robert Peel to power, in 1842, was a circumstance of some importance to the Bank of England. The powerful majority by which he was supported rendered it almost undoubted that he would maintain the position in which he had been placed by the country, when the expiration of the first ten years allowed by the charter for the continuance of the privileges of the corporation should arrive. It was almost equally certain that he would modify the principles on which it had hitherto been founded, according to his own views of the necessities of the monetary world. The Bank Act of 1844, marked an important era in the management and business of the Bank of England.

On each renewal of the charter the management sought to have incorporated in the laws for its government more liberal provisions than were accorded to or asked by any other banking institution. In some instances the bank was successful. Although a private enterprise, the Bank of England is generally regarded as a literal cog in the wheel of England's financial machinery.

Perhaps nowhere in the world does the history of banking show greater instability than in England, where during this century joint-stock banks have failed by the scores. Their profits in many instances have been very large, but their risks being correspondingly great, their failures have been most disastrous. Greater freedom has always existed in Scotch banking than in that of England, and consequently there has been greater security—those institutions, unlike the great monopoly, trading upon their capital.

The fluctuating and vascillating course pursued by the bank and its managers had attracted the attention of a number of able financial writers, prominent of whom were Lord Overstone, Colonel Torrens, Mr. Norman, and others.

They maintained and enunciated the following principles:—

1.—That bank notes, i. e., the promise of bankers to pay money on demand, alone are "currency," and that no other forms of paper credit are currency.

2.—That if banks are permitted to issue notes they ought to be only exactly in amount to what the specie would have been if there were no notes.

3.—That any excess of notes above the specie they displace is a depreciation of the currency.

The above named writers being men of great influence, converted Sir Robert Peel to their views, and on the renewal of the charter of the bank in 1844, Sir Robert Peel, then prime minister, having become satisfied of the dangerous influence exerted in the bank's ever varying and never stable system, first of expansion and then of contraction, in its laws, thought to provide a remedy. The principal feature of this measure was to limit the circulation so that it would be regulated by the amount of coin and bullion in the vaults of the institution.

Accordingly, he brought in a bill which became a law on July 19, 1844, entitled "An act to regulate the issue of bank notes, and for giving to the governor and company of the Bank of England certain privileges for a limited period."

In a speech in the House of Commons on May 6, 1844, on the renewal of the bank charter, Sir Robert Peel said:—

"With respect to the banking business of the bank, I propose that it should be governed on precisely the same principles as would regulate any other body dealing with Bank of England notes.   *   *   *   *   *

"It is said the Bank of England will not have the means which it has heretofore had of supporting public credit, and of affording assistance to the mercantile world in times of commercial difficulty. Now, in the first place, the means of supporting credit are not means exclusively possessed by banks. All who are possessed of unemployed capital, whether bankers or not, and who can gain an adequate return by the advance of capital, are enabled to afford, and do afford, that aid which it is supposed by some that banks alone are enabled to afford. In the second place, it may be a question whether there be any permanent advantage in the maintenance of private or public credit, unless the means of obtaining it are derived from the *bona fide* advance of capital, and not from a temporary increase of promissory notes issued for a special purpose. Some apprehend that the proposed restrictions upon issue will diminish the power of the bank to act with energy at the period of monetary crisis and commercial alarm and derangement; but the object of the measure is to prevent (so far as legislation can prevent) the recurrence of those evils from which we suffered in 1825, 1836, and 1839. It is better to prevent the paroxysm than to excite it, and trust to desperate remedies for the means of recovery."

The machinery adopted was as follows: The bank was divided into two departments. The Issue Department, and the Banking Department.

Following is the law as finally enacted for the guidance of the Bank of England:

1.—Provides for "the issue department of the Bank of England," which shall provide the notes payable on demand, and shall, from August 31, 1844, be kept wholly separate and distinct.

2.—That on August 31, 1844, the bank shall transfer to the issue department securities to the value of fourteen millions, the debt due by the public to be deemed part; that the banking department shall transfer to the issue department all the gold coin and gold and silver bullion not required; that the issue department shall deliver to the banking department such an amount of notes as with those in circulation shall equal the securities, coin, and bullion transferred to the issue department;

that the bank may not increase, but diminish the amount and again increase it to any sum not exceeding fourteen millions.

3.—That the bank shall not retain in its issue department at one time silver to any amount greater than one-fourth the gold held at the same time.

4.—That notes may be demanded for gold bullion at the rate of £3 17s. 9d. per oz. of standard gold.

5.—Provides for a weekly statement of the affairs of the bank.

6.—That the bank shall be exempt from stamp duty on its notes.

7.—That the bank allow £180,000 per annum out of the amounts payable by government for the exclusive privileges of banking.

8.—That the public shall receive such profits as may be obtained by an increase of circulation, beyond the amount provided in paragraph 2.

9.—That no other banks of issue be allowed, but such as were in existence May 6, 1844.

10.—That no bank in England or Wales shall issue any bill of exchange or promissory. note payable on demand, excepting such bankers as were in existence May 6, 1844. That no company now consisting of six or less than six partners shall, if they exceed that number, be allowed to issue notes.

By an Act passed the same year, with reference to joint-stock banks in England, so many restrictive clauses were introduced as practically to prevent any new institutions of the kind from being established. Since then more liberal measures have been enacted recognizing limited liability, and under it many institutions are in successful operation throughout the United Kingdom.

It is needless to recapitulate the various Acts of Parliament which affected the Bank of England during the first one hundred and fifty years of its existence. Its operations were yearly assuming greatly increased proportions. The Act of 1844, which regulated the bank note issues of the country, also prescribed the conditions in accordance with which the bank is now conducted.

A minute and extended discussion of the provisions of the Act would not be particularly interesting or instructive, but those parts which affect the constitution of the bank are :—

1st. Those which created the "Issue Department," by means of which the issue of notes is distinctly separated from the Banking Department.

2d. Those limiting the issue of notes to such a sum as the bank may hold in bullion (of which a fifth part may be silver), in addition to a sum of £14,000,000, increased since that date to £16,200,000, issued on securities, whereof the debt due by the public to the Bank formed part.* And,

3rd. Those compelling the bank to purchase any amount of gold offered to it at a certain fixed rate ; or, in other words, to receive in deposit any quantity of gold at a certain rate in exchange for bank notes.

The Act by this means secures, as far as possible, that gold shall be the basis of the currency of the country,

---

* The Act of 1844, which limited the note issue of the then existing private Banks, provided that when any Issuing Bank relinquished its right of issue, the Bank of England might increase its issue on securities in a fixed proportion to the amount thus withdrawn.

the note circulation expanding or contracting as gold in plentiful or scarce, or as if it consisted of gold only; and also acts as a guarantee to the general note-holder for the convertibility of his note. This last is assured by the special constitution of the Issue Department, where the right is confirmed of demanding at any moment coin for notes; and, further, by the weekly publication of the accounts of this department, which explain at a glance, and in the simplest language, that the issue of the notes is the same as the bullion of which the bank is possessed in this department, plus the £16,200,000 issued on securities.

For the privileges in regard to the issuing of bank notes, and for exemption from duty on them, the bank now pays to Government a sum of £213,895 per annum. The bank, however, makes no additional profit on any issue beyond £14,000,000. Although the amount on which notes are issued on security has been raised to £16,200,000, the profit on the additional sum accrues under the Act of 1844, to the public, and hence it is evident that the cost of every note issued beyond the sum of £16,200,000 is a direct charge on the bank for the benefit and convenience of the public.

It was eventually demonstrated that Robert Peel entirely misapprehended the causes at work in producing the fluctuations complained of, and that he applied the restrictions to that particular branch which varied but little in a series of years. The real cause of the trouble was to be found in the loans; which have been irregular in the extreme and at times productive of great injury. This injury has not alone been confined to Great Britain, but has extended in a greater or less degree to every country with which intimate business relations existed. That the Peel Act had no effect in mitigating the evil, will be clearly seen in the fact that these fluctuations have never been more violent than since its passage. The British public had long shown entire confidence in the circulating medium, and no legislation to effect this object was necessary. Since the passage of the law it has several times been suspended, as no doubt it will be again whenever it is rendered necessary to do so. One of the suspensions was on May 11, 1866, on which day the bank raised the rate of discount, to 10 per cent., it having been 6 per cent. nine days before. It its efforts to save itself and comply with the absurd provisions of the bank act, it spread ruin and desolation around it, and years have been necessary to enable the country to recover from the effects of the panic thus created. While the notes of the bank are legal tender elsewhere, they are not such in payments by the bank itself.

The notes of the Bank of England in circulation for some years previously to 1844 rarely amounted to twenty, or sunk so low as sixteen millions. And such being the case, Sir Robert Peel was said to be justified in assuming that the circulation of the bank could not, in any ordinary condition of society, or under any merely commercial vicissitudes, be reduced below fourteen millions. The law of 1844 allowed the bank to issue this amount upon securities, of which the £11,015,100 lent by the bank to the public was the most important item. Inasmuch, however, as the issues of the provincial banks were at the same time limited in their amount, and confined to certain existing banks, it was further provided, in the event of any of these banks ceasing to issue notes, that the Bank of England might be empowered, by order in council, to issue, upon securities, two-thirds, and no more, of the notes which such banks had been authorized to issue. Under this condition the total secured issue of the bank was increased. But for every other note which the issue department may at any time issue over and above the maximum amount issued on securities, an equal amount of coin or bullion must be paid into its coffers.

It will be seen that under this system the notes of the Bank of England were rendered really and truly equivalent to gold, while their immediate conversion into that metal no longer depends, as it previously did, on the good faith, the skill, or the prudence of the directors. These important results have been attained without imposing any burden of which anyone has any right to complain. English currency rests on the fundamental principle that all debts above forty shillings must be paid in gold. But individuals and associations, including the banking or commercial department of the bank, have the option, if they prefer it, to exchange gold for bank-notes, and to make use of the latter in their dealings with the public. Hence, if A or B goes to the issuers of paper, and gets 100 or 500 notes from them in exchange for an equivalent amount of gold, it is his own convenience he has exclusively in view. He was at full liberty to use gold, but he preferred exchanging it for notes because he could employ the latter more advantageously. This is the way in which paper is issued under the act of 1844; and such being the case it is contradictory to say that it is productive either of hardship or inconvenience. It certainly is a wise Act.

It is alleged that the new system is injurious by shackling the bank in the use of its credit, and the answer given is, that it does this in order to prevent the greater injury of over-issues of paper. The law very properly prevents the bank from issuing substitutes for money which does not represent money. It does not absorb or lock up a single sixpence worth of capital, nor does it interfere in any manner of way with its employment. The gold in the issue department of the Bank of England was not purchased by the bank and does not belong to it! The bank is its keeper, but not its owner. It belongs to the public, or to the holders of bank notes, who deposited it in the bank in exchange for notes, with and under the express stipulation, that on paying the latter into the bank they should receive back their gold. Any interference with these deposits would be an interference with property held in pledge for others, that is, it would be an act precisely of the same kind with that which exposes private bailees to penal servitude.

But though the bank directors may not lay violent hands on the property of the public, the bank, it is obvious, has at this moment the same absolute command over its entire capital and credit, that it would have were the Act of 1844 non-existent.

Beginning on page 271 will be found the full correspondence between the Chancellor of the Exchequer and the Bank of England relative to the renewal of the bank charter in 1844.

CHAPTER X.

RADICAL CHANGES IN THE MANAGEMENT OF THE BANK.

Privileges of Officers and Directors—Groundless Nature of a Charge Often Made—Plausible Objections to New Laws—Amount of Notes Issued—How to Determine an Excess of Currency—Notes in the Banking Department—Great Changes Wrought in the Management of the Bank—Restricting Banks for the Issuing of Notes—Convertibility of Bank of England Notes—Variations in the Rate of Discount—Temporary Suspension of the Act of 1844 to Avert a Panic—Effect of Modification of Usury Laws—Particulars as to Number and Class of Depositors—Development of the Methods of Economizing Money—Transitory Credits—Discount Variations—Credit and Capitalists—No Change Probable in the Methods of the Bank of England—Should Banks be Prohibited From Issuing Notes—True Way to Remove Danger—Modification of Banking Laws—Bank of England Notes Made Legal Tender.

APART from the practice of issuing transferable notes, the Bank of England is free from all restraint, and is in precisely the same situation as other banking or mercantile establishments. Its directors may lend or not lend as they please, and may lay down such conditions as they please in regard to the interest and the terms of loans and discounts. In short, they may do whatever they like with their own; but farther they are not permitted to go. They may not substitute shadows for realities. They cannot, whether to assist others, or to relieve themselves from embarrassment, issue a single note except upon a deposit of bullion. But this rule does not operate on the bank only. It applies to all individuals and associations. And to relax it in any degree would be—disguise it as one may—to authorize an issue of fictitious or spurious paper, and consequently to vitiate the currency and to abuse credit in the way that is sure to be in the end the most disastrous.

This statement shows the groundless nature of the charge which is often made against the Act of 1844, (which is given in preceding chapter) that under its operation the bank runs the risk of being brought to a stop, though it may have some five, six, or even eight millions bullion in its coffers. For it is plain that two things are confounded in this charge, which are quite distinct, and have no necessary connection with each other, viz., the proceedings of the bank in the capacity of issuer of notes, and its proceedings in the capacity of a banking company. In the former capacity it is all but impossible that it should be brought to a stop; and if such a thing should happen, there would not then be an ounce of bullion in its coffers. It is not, however, impossible nor even very improbable, that the bank should be brought, in its mercantile capacity, into difficulties, while there may be a large amount of bullion in the issue department. But, though such should be the case, is that any reason why the bank directors should be permitted to draw on funds that do not belong to them, and over which they have no control? Supposing the bank was in difficulties, is it to be allowed to right itself by setting aside the principle of *meum* and *tuum*, and seizing on what belongs to others? The directors would be the first to repudiate such a doctrine, which must be rejected by all men who have any sense of honor or regard for character.

One of the most plausible objections to the Act of 1844 is that it "limits the currency;" that it makes no provision for the increasing demands of the public; and confines matters in 1888, when the exports are in the hundreds of millions, to the same amount of money as in 1844, when the exports did not exceed 58½ millions. The simple truth, however, is that the Act allows money to be imported and exported, to be retained or sent elsewhere, just as it is wanted, and what it does limit is the uncontrolled issue of paper representatives of money, which experience proved were too often omitted without any reference to the reserves of money kept to maintain the convertibility of the paper issued. The £16,200,000 now issued on securities is the only thing that is limited in the Act; everything else varies with the varying condition and circumstances of the country, including the means by which the use of money may be economized.

The present note issue of the Bank of England, October, 1888, is £36,829,970; notes in circulation £23,142,180; estimated average circulation for 1888, £24,381,000. And if the country had really required a larger supply of money, that is, if more coins, or paper equivalent to coins, could have been absorbed into the circulation without rendering the currency redundant, and depressing the exchange, the additional quantity would have been forthwith supplied. For, under such circumstances, merchants, bankers, and money-dealers, would have realized a certain and immediate profit by carrying bullion to the mint or the bank, that they might obtain coins, or notes, or both, with which to increase the currency. It is one of the chief merits of the Act of 1844, that, under its agency, the supply of money is not to any extent or in any degree regulated or influenced by the proceedings of the bank or the Government. They have nothing to do in the matter, unless it be to coin the bullion which individuals or firms carry to the mint for that purpose, and to exchange, when called upon, notes for coins, and coins for notes. The supply of money, like that of all non-monopolized articles, is wholly dependent upon, and is determined by the free action of the public. It would, indeed, be quite as true to say, that the Act of 1844 limits the amount of corn, of cloth, or of iron produced in the country, as that it limits the amount of money. It maintains the value of the notes issued by the bank on a level with the coins for which they are substitutes; but beyond that its effect is *nil*. It has nothing whatever to do with the greater or less amount of the coin and notes of trustworthy convertibility put into circulation. That depends entirely on the estimate formed by the public of its excess or deficiency, an estimate which when wrong is sure to be corrected by the exchanges.

It may be added, that no inference can ever be safely

drawn from the number of notes or coins, or both, afloat in a country, as to whether its currency be, or be not, in excess. That is to be learned by the state of the exchange, or by the influx and efflux of bullion. If the imports of bullion exceed the exports, it shows that the currency is in some degree deficient; while, if the exports exceed the imports, it shows that the currency is in excess, and that no additions can be made to it without farther depressing the exchange and increasing the drain of bullion. When the imports and exports of bullion are about equal, then of course the currency is at about its proper level. These are the only criteria by which anything can ever be correctly inferred in regard to the deficiency or excess of currency. Its absolute amount affords hardly even a basis for conjecture. When there is little speculation or excitement, an issue of 25 or 27 millions bank notes may be in excess; while, at another time, and with a different state of trade and speculation, an issue of 35 or 37 millions of notes may not be enough. Except in periods of internal commotion, or when the country is disturbed by alarms of invasion, the state of the exchange is the only, as it is the infallible, test of the sufficiency and insufficiency of the currency. We may further state, that those who are in the habit of complaining of the limitation of the currency by the Act of 1844, almost uniformly underrate its amount. We have already seen that the notes issued by the issue department of the bank in October, 1888, amounted to £36,829,970, and of these £13,687,795 were in the banking department of the bank, leaving a balance of £23,142,180 in the hands of the general public; and this latter sum is, we are told, the real amount of the issues. But this is falling into the rather serious blunder of mistaking a part for the whole. The notes in the banking department of the bank make not only a part, but a most important and active part, of the currency of the country. They constitute the means, along with the bullion in the same department, with which the bank carries on her banking business, and are as evidently a portion of the currency as the notes in the tills of private bankers and the pockets of individuals. The notes in the banking department of the bank must therefore never be omitted in estimating the amount of notes in circulation. The latter, and the notes out of the issue department, are identical; and, in a general point of view, it matters not a straw whether they are in the hands of the banking department of the bank or of individuals.

So far the legislation of 1844 in its direct bearing on the Bank of England has been specifically treated. It will be found the most interesting and instructive move in the life of the world's greatest financial institution. Sir Robert Peel was unable to complete the full routine of his policy, but his action wrought wonderful changes.

He held that experience had shown that the balance of advantages lay on the side of suppression of all note issues except that of the Bank of England, as reformed by him, or of some similar supplementary establishments regulated in the same manner. But it was obviously impossible to prohibit, without compensation, the future exercise by country bankers of the rights they had legitimately acquired; and as it was not easy to buy up the existing privileges of the private and joint-stock banks, Sir Robert Peel allowed them to remain under conditions prohibiting their extension, and he apparently hoped that country issues would gradually disappear before the rivalry of Bank of England notes. The Act of 1844, accordingly, enacted that no new bank for the issue of notes should be established in any part of the United Kingdom; and that the *maximum* issue of notes by the existing country banks of England should in future be limited to the average amount which they had respectively in circulation during the twelve weeks preceding the 27th of April, 1844. It was also ordered that the names of the partners in joint-stock and other banks should be periodically published. A provision was also enacted under which an issuing bank could resign its privilege by composition with the Bank of England. The existing law was maintained preventing the issue of any notes other than the Bank of England in London, and the establishment, within sixty-five miles of London, of any branch of an English joint-stock bank having the privilege of issue.

The convertibility of the Bank of England notes has been perfectly maintained since 1844; and the management of English banks, whether private or joint-stock, has been sound and judicious, the cases of failure among them being few and contrasting strongly with the recurrent epidemics of insolvency of earlier experience. It must, however, be admitted that the variations in the rate of discount charged by the bank have been much more numerous and violent since 1844 than they were before, and on three occasions—in 1847, 1857, 1866—it has been judged necessary to authorize a suspension of the Act so far as to allow the bank directors the power to strengthen the banking department by recourse to the reserves of the issue department. In each case the suspension of the Act arrested and allayed the panic prevailing up to the moment of suspension, and in 1866 it was not, in fact, found necessary to exercise the power to borrow from the issue department which had been conceded to the directors.

It is necessary to enquire whether the Act of 1844 is to be blamed for the increase in the number of changes of the rate of discount which has since been experienced, and whether this increase and the suspension of the Act in time of trial constitute a reason for its abrogation or for a modification of its provisions. In the first place, the increased number of changes in the rate of discount is more apparent than real. The management of the Bank of England has become responsive to the movement in the value of money in the open market in a degree unknown before this generation. The rate of discount outside the bank changed rapidly and often before 1844, but its fluctuations were to a large extent prevented from affecting the Bank of England. Previously to the modification of the Usury Laws in 1839, the bank could not charge more for loans than five per cent., and for some considerable period after the restriction had been removed the directors, influenced, in part at least, by their accustomed habit on several occasions, permitted the bank to be involved in difficulties which might have been averted by the sooner raising the rate of discount.

Strict limitation in the number and class of customers with whom the bank would do business, and a refusal to rediscount bills that had been already discounted by money dealers, made it possible to keep the bank rate below the rates of the open market without exposing the resources of the establishment to an exhausting demand.

Next, it is to be observed that the methods of economizing the use of money by the development of banking have been extraordinarily multiplied during the past few years. The Bank Act, as has been shown, in no way operates to diminish the supply of money in the country; on the contrary, it tends to increase it, since it forbids any extension of the use of notes issued on credit as a substitute for money. The effect of the Act has therefore been to neutralize rather than to stimulate the process of economy in the use of money to which we have called attention. But the transactions of bankers—the issue of checks, the negotiation of bills, etc., etc., have multiplied out of all proportion to the stock of ready money on which they risk, and the mass of transitory credits being constantly increasing while the reserves of cash suffer little change, there naturally and necessarily follows an increased sensibility in the equilibrium of the money market, with constant oscillations in the rate of interest. But although the increase in the number of changes of discount since 1844 has not been as great as may at first seem apparent, and so far as the increase has been real it must be chiefly attributed to the growing disproportion between the magnitude of transitory credits at any time existing and the reserve of cash kept on hand, yet it may be freely admitted that it is not impossible that changes have from time to time happened that might not have occurred supposing the separation of the banking and issue departments had not been established. It is evident that if the cash in the two departments had been equally accessible to the bank directors, a withdrawal of money which is now thrown upon one department would not have caused so great a change in the proportion between liabilities and reserve.

The oscillations experienced in the rate of discount in the Bank of England, oscillations which after all indicate nothing more than the natural movement in the value of a medium which is the first to be agitated by changes in value of every other commodity, are cheaply purchased as the price of the permanent and perfect equality of the bank note and the money it represents. The repeated suspensions of the Act of 1844 in time of trial do, *prima facie*, present a much stronger argument for the repeal of the statute. Legislation which breaks down upon critical occasions discredits the legislature that decreed it; and it is not to be denied that the mere suspension of the Act has more than once operated as a charm to allay feelings of panic among bankers, money dealers, and merchants. It must also be admitted that Sir Robert Peel, in common with the earlier advocates of the policy of the Act, believed that it would prevent the recurrence of commercial crises. It is strange that such an anticipation should have been entertained.

Whoever will reflect on the nature of the organization of credit in the commercial world, and on the timid and self protecting instincts of men, especially of capitalists, will be forced to confess that the recurrence of crises must be accepted as inevitable. The more highly developed is the economy of money the greater must be the sum which banks and bankers are liable to be called upon to repay on demand or at short notice in proportion to the reserves of money kept in their coffers; and the greater also must be the amount of bills falling due daily, and largely met as they fall due by the proceeds of bills drawn daily and discounted as drawn. The smoothness of action of the commercial machine evidently depends upon the continuance of that confidence which is ordinarily felt by the creditor class in the solvency of debtors, and any access of distrust may easily produce consequences culminating in a crisis. Bankers who are at once debtors and creditors are necessarily constrained to protect themselves in such periods of defective confidence by declining to meet the applications for loans and discounts which are forced upon them; and a sharp competition ensues for the possession of the ready money that is available in the market. The pressure is concentrated upon the Bank of England, and the publicity of the condition of that institution, consequent upon the weekly issue of its balance sheet, lets all men know the rate of decline of its cash reserve. At such a time an accident may cause the spirit of caution to pass into apprehension and panic. The fear that the cash balances of the banking department may be exhausted incites bankers to hasten to anticipate one another in withdrawing any reserve they may have kept at the bank, and the rate of diminution of the cash of the department is accelerated. It is obvious that the condition we have described is in its origin independent of any particular regulations adopted with respect to the note circulation of a community; and it has, in fact, been experienced in Great Britain under all varieties of laws, and in the United States, in Northern and Southern Germany, and in the British colonies under an equally wide dissimilarity of currency-regulations. English history shows that such a condition may be aggravated, if not precipitated, by an antecedent issue of notes increasing the proportion between the volume of transitory credits and the cash available to meet instantaneous demands; and as long as the issue of notes was unrestricted, bankers could never resist the temptation to make up, by an increase in their issues, any diminution in their available cash, a cause directly provocative of a further diminution by its effect on adverse exchanges, and therefore producing a sharper reaction when the necessity was at last recognized of recovering the balance between their cash in hand and their liabilities. No legislation can prevent panic, but it prevents bankers from resorting to causes which aggravate panics, and it moreover supplies a means of allaying the unreasoning terror in which panics culminate. Were it not for the separation of the issue and banking departments we should be constrained to witness and tolerate periodical suspension of cash payments, as this would be the only means left of appeasing alarm; and this desperate expedient has been, in fact, employed over and over again, under such circumstances, both in England and elsewhere.

When the minds of creditors are unhinged, and all are competing for money which is not in existence in sufficient quantities to satisfy their demands, the announcement that the Government has authorized the bank directors to suspend the action of the Act and to fall back on the resources of the issue department operates as a charm. The mere announcement is often enough to put an end to the panic previously prevailing, the feverish fit passes away, and the customary temper of confidence is more or less slowly restored.

It is said that the existence of the Act of 1844 is justified even when it is suspended, for it provides, in the maintenance of the cash reserves of the issue department, a stock of money, the unlocking of which furnishes the means of arresting panic which would otherwise have to be sought in a periodic suspension of cash payments. It has naturally been asked whether the law might not be saved the apparent discredit involved in its being set aside by an act of the Executive Government, acting on the faith of a subsequent indemnity from Parliament, by the embodiment in it of a power authorizing its suspension under circumstances that provoke its suspension.

We have already said that Sir Robert Peel contemplated an ultimate extinction of all note issues save that of the Bank of England; and he probably expected that the substitution of Bank of England notes for all others would not be long delayed. The progress actually achieved towards this end has been very slow. It may be added that the provisions of the Act of 1844, relied upon Sir Robert Peel for bringing about by arrangement a substitution of Bank of England notes for those of privileged bankers, have been for many years entirely neglected. With these facts before us it is not surprising that, in 1866, Mr. Gladstone, as Chancellor of the Exchequer under Lord Palmerston, should have submitted to the House of Commons a bill dealing with the subject. By it, it was proposed that private banks of issue in England and Wales should be released from the existing restriction that the numbers of partners must not exceed six, and that joint-stock banks should be allowed to come within the circle of sixty-five miles from London upon their undertaking to pay annually to the Exchequer a duty at the rate of one per cent., and on their average issues, and that thereupon their privileges of issue should be assured to them until 1890, at which time they should cease. The bill was purely permissive; but it was thought by its author that a large proportion of the English banks of issue would place themselves under its operation, and further legislation would be practicable with respect to the rest. The bill, however, was less and less approved as it became better known, and it was ultimately withdrawn.

There is no probability of any legislation being enacted, supposing legislation to be desirable, looking to a radical change in the methods of the Bank of England or the strong private and joint-stock banks of the Kingdom. The reasons for this are many, the chief, however, being the fact that the bankers of the Kingdon are largely represented on both sides of the House of Commons, and they are on the whole quite well contented with the present state of the law, while the great body of the public are profoundly ignorant, and uninterested in it. In America, banks are plenty and banking business so general that nearly every intelligent citizen takes a direct and positive interest in banks and banking, and as a natural outcome of this public censorship beneficial and equitable legislation is easily enacted whenever necessary.

In England, the inaction to overcome is so great, and the force available is so limited, nothing will be done except under the influence of a commercial crisis, when almost anything can be done. The aim of economists and statesmen should be to produce a body of authority that may command respect even in the midst of universal agitation.

At the risk of stating something that may appear too obviously true to require statement, we would submit that the question, whether bankers should be permitted to issue notes, must be determined upon a balance of opposing considerations of expediency. Many of the advocates and supporters of Sir Robert Peel's legislation of 1844, have said, apparently with a conviction that they were expressing an axiomatic truth, that the issue of notes was no part of the business of a banker. The force of assertions of this kind cannot be admitted by everybody. There is certainly no law of nature limiting the action of a banker within the bounds sought to be prescribed; and if we accept as the definition of a banker a person whose business it is to borrow and lend money, we cannot but recognize in the issue of transferable notes a most convenient process of carrying on this business.

A banker who issues notes borrows so much from the persons from time to time holding them, and this money he has lent to the customers indebted to him. The reasons of convenience which justify a prohibition of the liberty of issue are,

FIRST.—That experience has shown that this process of borrowing is too patent and too easily abused to the precipitation and aggravation of commercial crises.

SECOND.—That the great and almost insuperable difficulty of refusing to receive notes which have obtained general currency makes it most desirable that such notes should possess some better guarantee than can be always forthcoming of the solvency of private issuers.

These are the reasons which prevail to uphold Sir Robert Peel's legislation, and which impel one to consider what means may be discovered of perfecting his policy by the unification of issuers throughout the Kingdom.

The time when one note currency, and the acceleration of the time when one currency only shall be in circulation, would both be greatly facilitated by a mechanical and local separation of the issue department from the Bank of England. Much confusion of thought still prevails by reason of the fact that the Bank of England is used as the agent for managing what is now a state issue, resting, so far as it is uncovered by specie, upon state security.

If the business of issuing notes were removed bodily from the Bank of England and located in a Government office, and the name of the notes at the same time changed, it could not fail to be seen that the business left behind in Threadneedle street differed in no essential particular from that of any other banker in Lombard street, and much of the superstitious regard for the Bank of England, and trust in its assistance in time of trouble, would be rapidly destroyed. It would then be understood that the cry for ministerial interference at the time of crises, and of incipient crises, was nothing more than a claim for the nation to cover with its credit those who had not been prudent enough to maintain adequate reserves for their own defence; and, as this would be understood beforehand, it would induce the consequence of greater circumspection on the part of dealers in money and a less temptation to rely on extraneous aid. The purely mechanical act of removing the issue of notes from

Threadneedle street would make the facts of the situation plain, and would bring about an alteration of conduct among London bankers, so that it should conform to the facts thus perceived.

The cash reserves kept by the London bankers are disproportionately small compared with the amount of their instantaneous liabilities. Competition has, of course, been a considerable element in causing this attenuation of cash reserves. Each joint-stock bank has struggled after that increase of credit which follows an increase of dividends; and the unproductive cash balances on hand have been kept down to the lowest limit. They would, however, never have been reduced to such narrow dimensions but for the reliance placed on the assistance of the Bank of England in the last extremity; and if it were made plain that the Bank of England is itself nothing more than a big joint-stock bank, this reliance would disappear. Many schemes, equally ingenious and chimerical, have been recently put forth for compelling bankers to keep larger reserves of cash in proportion to their deposits. The true way to remove the danger that is always threatening, under the system that exists, is to produce a conviction among bankers that they must not expect help elsewhere if they become distressed through a default in their own reserves of cash.

If the separation of the issue department from the rest of the Bank of England was completed by its transfer to a Government office under the management of state agents, the unification of the issues of the Kingdom might be accomplished by legislation akin to that adopted by the United States in relation to the national banks. Each bank of issue might be required to withdraw its own notes and to receive and put out in exchange for them notes emanating from the state establishment, but bearing a statement on their face of the banks through which they were issued. Government securities should be deposited by the issuing banks for the amounts thus put into circulation, which must not exceed the amount of their existing authorized issues ; and the interest on these securities would be paid to the banks, less a fixed charge to defray the cost of preparing and issuing the notes delivered to them. The notes thus issued would be payable at the central state office, and would circulate throughout the kingdom ; but as often as they were brought back to the central office they would be cleared again by the several issuing banks for reissue, unless the latter desired to be retired from the arrangement, in which case the issuing bank would redeem the notes it issued, which would be cancelled, and the securities deposited, or a corresponding part of them, would be handed back. It would not be improper to force this plan on the acceptance of the privileged banks of issue, although it is believed it would be freely accepted, inasmuch as their notes would at once acquire currency throughout the kingdom without discrimination of locality in exchange for the deposit of security, and the gain they now realize from the issue of notes would be left undiminished.

Up to the year 1858, banking companies could not be constituted with limited liability of partners except by way of privilege under special Acts of Parliament ; and although the Bank of England, and the three oldest established banks in Scotland, were thus favored without any consequent deterioration in the character of their management, abundant arguments were adduced in depreciation of a general law on the subject. In 1858, however, an Act was passed authorizing the formation and registration of banking companies with limited liability, and also enabling existing unlimited companies to register as associations with a limited liability of partners, subject to a proviso that if the bank was a bank of issue, the liability of its partners should remain unlimited in respect of such issue. Several banks have been established and registered under this law, and no evil results have been observed to follow.

When the charter was renewed in 1833, the notes of the Bank of England were made legal tender everywhere in England, except at the bank. Of the wisdom of this regulation no doubt can be entertained. Bank notes are necessarily always equivalent to bullion; and, by making them substitutes for coin at country banks, the demand for the latter during periods of alarm or runs is materially diminished, and the stability of the bank and of the pecuniary system of the country proportionately increased.

CHAPTER XI.

FRAUDS, FORGERIES, THEFTS AND DEFALCATIONS.

The First Forged Note on the Bank of England and Execution of the Forger—How Discovered—Counterfeiting—Decision of the Lord Chief Justice—Defeating Counterfeiters—Great Theft of the Head Cashier of the Bank of England—A Loss of £320,000—Inventing a Safety Paper—Men Executed by Scores for Counterfeiting—Ingenious Schemes for Swindling—Sir Robert Peel Victimised—Another Thieving Official—Fauntleroy Secures £360,000 by Forgery—A Rascally Clerk Escapes to the United States and is Apprehended—Losses by Forgery—A Chief Clerk Swindles the Bank to the Amount of £800,000—His Novel Method that went Undetected for Five Years—Bidwell's Million Pound Swindle.

LIKE all great monetary institutions, the Bank of England has been the victim of innumerable forgeries, thefts and defalcations by trusted servants and wily rogues.

The day on which a forged note was first presented at the Bank of England forms a memorable era in its history. For sixty-four years the establishment had circulated its paper with freedom; and during this period no attempt had been made to imitate it. He who takes the initiative in a new line of wrongdoing has more than the simple act to answer for, and to Richard William Vaughan, a linen draper, belongs the melancholy celebrity of having led the van in this new phrase of crime, in the year 1758. The records of his life do not show want, beggary, or starvation urging him to crime, but a foolish desire to seem greater than he was. By one of the engravers employed, and there were several employed on different parts of the notes, the fraud was discovered. The rascal had filled up to the number of twenty, and deposited them in the hands of a young lady to whom he was attached, as a proof of his wealth. There is no calculating how much longer Bank of England notes might have been free from imitation, had this man not shown with what ease they might be counterfeited. From this period forged notes became common. The faculty of imitation is so great, that when the expectation of profit is added, there is little hope of restraining the destitute or a bad man from a career which adds the charm of novelty to the chance of gain. The publicity given to the fraud, the notoriety of the proceedings, and the execution of the forger, tended to excite that morbid sympathy which, up to the present day, is evinced for any extraordinary criminal. It is, therefore, possible that if Vaughan had not been induced by circumstances to startle London with his novel crime, the idea of forging bank notes might have been long delayed, and that some of the strange facts to be related would never have occurred.

The same year (1758) was also memorable for a judgment passed by the Lord Chief Justice, in connection with some notes which were stolen from the mails. The robber, after stopping the coach, and taking out all the money contained in the letters, went boldly to a neighboring post-office and had one of the notes exchanged. The remainder of the stolen notes were passed on tradesmen. They were, however, stopped at the bank, and an action was brought by the possessors to recover the money. The question attracted widespread attention, and it was decided by the law authorities:—"That any person paying a valuable consideration for a bank note, payable to bearer, in a fair course of business, has an undoubted right to recover the money from the bank."

The notes of a banking establishment are always liable to imitation; and as the paper of a national bank circulates as freely as coin, it is not surprising that men of desperate hopes have successfully attempted to gain by fraud that which they were denied by fortune.

John Mathison was a man of great mechanical capacity, who, becoming acquainted with an engraver, unhappily acquired that art which ultimately proved his ruin and cost him his life. A yet more dangerous qualification of his was imitating signatures with remarkable accuracy. In London he forged a large number of Bank of England notes, the paper, engraving, water-mark and general appearance being superior almost to the genuine. Having been in the habit of procuring notes from the bank, that he might the more accurately copy them, he chanced to be there when a customer paid in a number of guineas, one of which was scrupled. Mathison, from a distance, said it was a good one. "Then," said the bank clerk, on the trial, "I recollected him."

The frequent visits of Mathison, who was very incautious, together with other circumstances, created some suspicion that he might be connected with these notes. On another occasion, when Mathison was there, a forged note of his own was presented, and the teller, half in jest and half in earnest, charged Maxwell, the name by which Mathison was known, with some knowledge of the forgeries. Further suspicion was excited, and directions were given to detain him at some future period. The day following he was decoyed into the presence of the directors. To all inquiries he replied that he declined to answer; that he was a citizen of the world, and knew not how he had come into it, or how he should go out of it. He watched his chance, raised a window and dashed into the street. He was recaptured. His actions condemned him. Further questioning weakened him. He burst into tears, and yelling "I am a dead man," said he would confess all. At his trial he was found guilty on his own acknowledgement, when he stated he could make a whole note in one day. It was asserted at the time, that, had it not been for his confession, he could not have been convicted. He offered to explain the secret of his discovery of the water-mark, provided the bank officials would intercede with the Government to spare his life. His proposal was rejected, and he paid the penalty with his life.

Forgeries still continued. Considering the advances made in the mechanical arts, they were rough and even rude in their execution. Easily imitated, they were also easily circulated. From 1797 the executions for forgery of £1 notes augmented to an extent which bore no proportion to any other class of crime. During the six years prior to their issue there was but one capital conviction; during the four following years eighty-five lives were taken for counterfeiting. This enormous increase produced inquiry, which resulted in an Act "For the better prevention of the forgery of the notes and bills of exchange of persons carrying on the business of bankers." By this some stringent penalties were denounced against offenders; and a notice to the following effect was published in the London papers in September, 1801 :—"All the one and two pound notes issued by the Bank of England after this date, will, to prevent forgeries, be printed on a peculiar and purposely constructed paper."

This endeavor to repress crime fell sadly short of the necessity, owing to the great truth that punishment is not a sufficient preventative of crime; but that to teach men to be good is more effectual than to punish them for being bad. So long as the law was left to take its course, and no voice was heard save that of the victim, the justice which hung a man for a one pound note was unquestioned. Finally a change came.

The first instance of fraud in the present century was the defalcation of no less a person than Mr. Robert Astlett, cashier of the Bank of England. In the year 1803, Mr. Bish, a member of the stock exchange, was applied to by Cashier Astlett to dispose of some exchange bills. When they were delivered into Mr. Bish's hands he was greatly astonished to find not only that these bills had previously been in his possession, but that they had been also delivered to the bank. Surprised at this, he immediately opened a communication with the directors, which led to the discovery of the fraud and the arrest of Astlett.

All the bank officials had the most implicit faith in Astlett's honesty, and his theft produced the greatest consternation imaginable.

At Astlett's trial it was shown that the prisoner had been placed in sole charge of all exchequer bills brought to the bank, and it was his duty to deliver them in person to the directors, who counted them, and a receipt given to the cashier. The prisoner, from his acquaintance with business, had induced the directors to believe that he had handed them bills to the amount of £700,000, when they were only in possession of £500,000. So completely did the cashier deceive the directors, that two of the body vouched by their signatures for the delivery of the larger amount.

The cashier was tried for the felonious embezzlement of three bills of exchequer for £1,000 each. By a technical objection of his counsel the cashier was acquitted. He was detained, however, until the directors could cause a civil process to be issued against him. From this plan they departed, and Astlett was again tried for the criminal offence. The indictment this time charged him with the felonious embezzlement of property and effects of the Bank of England. He was found guilty this time and sentenced to death. The sentence, however, was not executed, and Astlett remained a prisoner in Newgate for many years. The bank sustained a loss through Cashier Astlett's thefts of £320,000.

Forgeries still continued, and executions occurred weekly. Finally a committee was appointed to inquire into and devise a method to prevent the forgery of bank notes. In January, 1819, the committee rendered its report. They stated that the directors of the Bank of England had furnished them with a detailed account of one hundred and eight projects and specimens of the originals for forger-proof notes, and of the imitation of the above ordered by the directors. The committee had communications from seventy outsiders who had ideas. They also examined forged notes of various kinds. They finally concluded that the greatest degree of safety would be in specially devised paper. The following is a description, from a contemporary authority, of the improved note:—

"A number of squares will appear in chequer work upon the note, filled with hair lines in elliptic curves of various degrees of eccentricity, the squares to be alternately of red and black lines; the perfect mathematical coincidence of the extremities of the lines of different colors on the sides of the squares will be effected by the arrangement of machinery of singular fidelity. But even with the use of this machinery a person who has not the key to the proper disposition would make millions of experiments to no purpose. Other obstacles to imitation will be also presented in the structure of the note; but this is the one principally relied upon. It is plain that any failure in the imitation will be manifest to the observation of the most careless; and the most skillful merchants who have seen the operation declare that the note cannot be imitated. The machine works with three cylinders, and the impression is made by small convex cylindrical plates."

In the ten first years of the present century, £106,061 were refused payment on the plea of forgery. In 1797, the entire cost for prosecuting forgeries was £1,500, and in the last three months of 1818 it was nearly £20,000. It was clear that the severity of punishment had not prevented the crime of forgery. The bank directors were blamed on all sides for their presumed apathy. Every person who had proposed a plan, and had it declined, joined the cry. Every disappointed adventurer, who had asked for bank capital to carry out his scheme, asserted that they had not inquired into the particulars but dismissed an excellent proposal without due consideration. It was eventually found out that to prevent a crime was better than to punish it. Education, intelligence and a note almost impossible to imitate has rendered forged Bank of England notes well nigh impossible. In April, 1820, forty men were held in London for counterfeiting, and men were hung in strings. From one or two manufactories issued most, if not all, the forged notes which were in circulation; and the manufacturer of thousands remained unsettled while the issuer of one was hung. They were sold to ignorant, uneducated, and almost irresponsible men, for a few shillings in the pound; and there was always a sufficient number urged by want, desire, or vice, to run the risk which accompanied their circulation. When a poor man was hung the public looked upon the act as a virtuous atonement for an awful deed. But when a banker or gentleman was found in danger of punishment, the morbid sympathy of the people was excited.

In 1822, another servant was recreant to his trust. William Turner, a clerk, was discovered to be the perpetrator of a very singular and intricate fraud. Records of internal treachery have not been plenty in the Bank of England. It was Turner's duty to place a certain amount to the credit of Sir Robert Peel. He increased Peel's credit to the extent of £10,000. Having secured the foundation of the object which he had in view, the next movement was to dispose of the amount which he had thus created by a single stroke of his pen. The second step was effected with almost as much facility as the first, by opening an account in the fictitious name of J. Renn, of Highgate, whom he credited to the amount of £10,000. A purchaser was found, the stock appeared to the credit of the seller, and the transfer was effected.

The fraud was accidentally discovered. Great difficulty in fastening the crime on Turner was occasioned by the fact that he had covered up his tracks and destroyed many evidences of his guilt. On the trial, as the only witness who was disposed to swear decidedly to the writing of the prisoner was answering the questions put to him, Turner whispered to his counsel, who immediately asked the witness:—" Do you believe the New Testament to be a revelation from God?" The witness hesitated, and the question was repeated. "Yes, I do," was the reply, uttered in a faint tone. He was, however, again pressed, and evidence being produced to prove that he had frequently avowed his disbelief, the prisoner's fate was greatly decided by the knowledge, and the jury returned a verdict of " Not Guilty."

Turner retained the money. He even had the audacity to visit the bank. With his ill-gotten money Turner went to Italy, purchased a fine villa on the shores of Lake Como. His stealing amounted to many thousands of pounds, more than originally discovered. He soon dissipated his property and returned to England. A retributive justice overtook him, as it overtakes mostly all who depart from the path of rectitude, and he died in an obscure street in London, in a cheap lodging house, in the greatest poverty.

From 1815 to 1823, the Bank of England lost £360,000 by what is known as the Fauntleroy forgeries. Henry Fauntleroy was a partner in a private banking house. He was only twenty-five years of age. He was joint-trustee in an account with some other gentlemen in the imperial three-per-cents. He forged a power of attorney for the sale of same. No doubt appears to have been excited at the bank. It passed the ordeal of the bank examinations. In the management of the trust some difficulties arose, and the only plan which could save the executors was to throw the property into chancery. Fauntleroy strenuously objected. In the course of the dispute, one of the trustees visited the bank and learned the fearful intelligence which first led to the discovery of a series of gigantic forgeries, so gigantic in their respect, and so unparalleled in their nature, as to border on the regions of fiction. Fauntleroy was arrested. Among his papers was found this unique document:—

"In order to keep up the credit of our house, I have forged powers of attorney, and have, thereupon, sold out all these sums, without the knowledge of my partners. I have given credit in the accounts for interest when it became due. The Bank of England first began to refuse our acceptances, and thereby destroyed the credit of our house. The bank shall smart for it.

"HENRY FAUNTLEROY."

True to his word, the bank suffered to the extent of £360,000. The crime excited the greatest interest. The public press teemed with his doings. He had a book containing a classified list of his forgeries. He was tried, convicted, and expiated his crime at Newgate amidst thousands of spectators. In 1832, capital punishment for counterfeiting was repealed.

In the month of October, 1841, London was startled with a rumor of a series of forgeries. It was stated that a large number of the exchequer bills then in the market were forged. Edward Beaumont Smith, chief clerk in the exchequer office for twenty-eight years, was arrested for the forgery. Smith had taken genuine bills and forged the proper signature. In every other respect they were genuine. Smith had two confederates. For five years did Smith carry on his forgeries without detection. Upwards of £800,000 were thus procured. As another proof that money wrongfully gained is easily lost, they lost nearly all upon the stock market. It was invariably stipulated that the very bills which were pledged should be returned when the money was repaid, or on other exchequer bills being given. In this manner the rascals escaped detection until boldness caused a suspicion which led to their apprehension. Smith and his accomplices were transported for life.

In 1845, William Burgess, a clerk, forged a note for £8,500, and fled to the United States. He was captured in Boston and returned to England and punished.

The losses occurring to the Bank of England from forged notes and other fraudulent documents have been commensurate with the greatness of its transactions.

Still, constant vigilance is the price of security from losses by designing and unscrupulous men. Forgeries and defalcations of late years are not numerous and wrongdoing of employees rare. The system of checks used in all departments renders mistakes almost impossible, and internal dishonesty so sure of instant detection that crookedness is rarely ever attempted.

At an average of the ten years ending with 1831, the bank lost through forgeries, £40,204 per year. Since then modern appliances has reduced this to almost nothing.

In 1872, the Bank of England was defrauded of nearly 1,000,000 pounds sterling, through the rascality of four American thieves, George and Austin Bidwell, George McDonald and Edward Hills. These men discovered an unguarded loop-hole in the banking department of the bank and concocted a scheme to take advantage of this to swindle them to the best of their ability. The bank was in the habit of receiving bills of exchange in deposit on account without verifying either the signatures or the acceptances, and stowing them away until they became due.

These men managed to secure the necessary introduction, and opened an account with the bank under an assumed name. They then had hundreds of bills of exchange printed on counterfeit plates, and flooded the Bank of England with these bills from all over the world, profusely signed and accepted, and the bank unhesitatingly cashed them and put the proceeds to the credit of the rascals, which were drawn out in ostensible business transactions in such a manner as not to excite the suspicion of the bank officials. On one occasion the rascals neglected to date the acceptance of two of the fraudulent bills. These were sent by the bank to the acceptors to supply the omission and the fraud was at once discovered and exposed. The four men were apprehended after an exciting chase by detectives, and upon trial were all given life sentences. George Bidwell was pardoned in 1888 and returned to the United States. The other men are still in prison although a determined effort is being made by their friends to obtain their release.

CHAPTER XII.

MANAGEMENT OF THE NATIONAL DEBT.

Management of all Other Stocks Held by the Bank—How the Work is Performed by the Bank of England—Stock Offices—Dividend Pay Office—Cheque Office—Unclaimed Dividends—Stock Office Library—Number of Books in Library—A Perfect System—178,000 Distinct Accounts—Register Office—Post Warrant Office—The Routine Work of Above Named Offices Described—Names of the Governors of the Bank of England from 1694 to 1888.

THE management of the national debt, and of all the other stocks which are inscribed at, and the interest on which is payable by, the bank of England, is conducted in the Department of the Chief Accountant, who is responsible for the due performance of the various duties. The work is divided into the following offices—*viz.*, Stock, Transfer, Dividend, Post Warrant, Cheque, Register Office, Unclaimed Dividend, and the Stock Office Library. Each of these is under the superintendence of a Principal and Deputy-Principal, and the whole of them are under the control of one head, called the Controller of Stock Offices, who again is under the Chief Accountant. A brief description of the work of the various offices having in charge the national debt and other public stocks will be found interesting.

STOCK OFFICE.—The bank, in its capacity of manager or account-keeper of the national debt, neither buys nor sells, although as bankers, or in their corporate capacity, they may buy or sell, as may any other stockholders. Buying and selling stock is carried on principally through the intervention of stock-brokers. A person wishes to buy £1,000 of a particular stock, say £3 per cent. consols; he applies to his stock-broker, who deals with a person called a stock-jobber, and having agreed as to the price, the broker sends to the bank a transfer ticket or request to have a certain amount of stock transferred from the name A, a seller, to B, a buyer.

One of the clerks of the bank, who attends to the stock transactions of all accounts beginning with letter A, refers to the ledger to see that such an amount of stock is on the account of A, and he then copies from the transfer ticket left by the broker, into a book called the transfer book, which consists of blank forms of transfer, printed according to the regulation of the Acts of Parliament, the name into which the stock of A is required to be placed. In the meantime the broker has prepared a document called the stock receipt, agreeing in the main particulars with the entry made in the transfer book; and when A comes to make the transfer (having previously been identified to the satisfaction of the bank), he signs the book, which is a formal discharge to the bank for that amount of stock, and the stock receipt, which is handed to B, the buyer, as an acknowledgement both for the money received in purchase of the stock, and a memorandum that the said amount of stock has been transferred to B. From that moment A ceases to have any control over that particular amount of stock. It is at once entered in the name of B, and B stands in the place of A, and can, in like manner, on being identified, deal with the stock by selling to C. It matters not into how many accounts A may wish to transfer his stock; for if, instead of selling the whole amount to B, he sells one-half, or £100, or sixpence, the same operation goes on with respect to that particular part, as if he were selling all the amount standing in his name. Each transfer is a perfect deed of conveyance, and, when completed, the transaction is entered in a journal, from which it is then posted in the ledger.

The dividends on all British government stock, except the £2 15s., and the £2 10s. per cent. annuities, are paid half-yearly, either in January and July, or April and October.

DIVIDEND OFFICE—Immediately previous to the first day of payment, the dividend books and the warrants are passed from the Transfer Offices into the Dividend Office. The books being arranged on the counter in alphabetical order, and the warrants deposited in drawers inside the counters, both are presided over by a numerous staff of clerks, whose duty it is to deliver the warrants to the stockholders as they appear to receive their dividends. The parties applying must name the amount of stock of which they may be possessed. If right, the applicant is required to sign the dividend book as an acknowledgement that the dividend warrant has been received, and the warrant for the amount is then handed to him.

In the Dividend Pay Office are paid the dividends on:—

1. British Government Funds (including Life Annuities, the warrants for which are prepared and issued by the National Debt Office, Old Jewry).
2. Indian Government Debt.
3. Indian Railways purchased by the Government.
4. Metropolitan Board of Works and City of London Debts.
5. Various Colonial and British Corporation Stocks.
6. Turkish Guaranteed Loan.
7. Bank Stock.

On some of these stocks the dividends are payable only by warrant, on others only by coupon.

The warrant answers the double purpose of being a cheque payable on demand, as well as a receipt; the coupon is payable to bearer, but must be left for examination three clear days before being paid. Postal Warrants are only paid through a banker, but warrants other than these, and coupons, are paid either through a banker, or over the counter, in notes or coin, as may be desired.

The work of this office has been largely augmented of late years, owing partly to the great additions made in colonial and corporation stocks, and the growing tendency to pay dividends quarterly instead of half-yearly. At the heaviest periods of the year, when as many as 50 clerks are employed, from 10,000 to 12,000 separate dividend warrants are paid in a single day, about 3,000 of these being presented at the counter for payment in notes and coin. Great care is required in the manipulation of both warrants and coupons. After examination and payment, the warrants are cancelled by a small portion being punched out, the form and position of the punch mark denoting the date on which the warrants were paid.

Dividends are now paid on 75 stocks; the warrants number about 400,000, and the coupons 350,000, representing a value of about £38,000,000, and a capital stock of about £900,000,000.

CHEQUE OFFICE—The warrants paid in the Dividend Office are handed over, day by day, to the Cheque Office. The duty of this office is to make up the amount of all the warrants passed to it, and see that they agree in the aggregate with the amount paid upon them by the Dividend Office. The warrants are from time to time sorted into numerical order (which brings them into alphabetical order), and are then entered in journals marked with letters corresponding to the stock ledgers. The total of these journals should agree with the amount paid as represented in the cash books.

UNCLAIMED DIVIDENDS—It must be obvious that from many causes amounts of stock, and the dividends thereon, will from time to time remain unclaimed. Persons die intestate, and the relatives are not aware, perhaps, that they were possessed of stock. Others leave the country, and, perhaps, never return. When such amounts have remained unclaimed for ten years, they are transferred to the account of the commissioners for the reduction of the national debt, but the persons entitled to same can make their claim good at any time and receive their money.

STOCK OFFICE LIBRARY—The Stock Office Library of the bank contains the old stock ledgers, transfer books, dividend books, power of attorney cases, and numerous other books and documents, from the establishment of the bank in 1694, commencing with the original of bank stock created at that early period, and embracing the various government stocks, and securities from the respective dates of their creation down to the present time. There are about 65,000 of these books and documents, which are all placed under the immediate charge of a librarian, and so systematically and conveniently arranged that reference can readily be made to any of them. They are all in good condition, and their due preservation is a matter of considerable moment. It is not too much to assert that the titles of all who have at any time been possessed of government stock, can be proved by these means readily. No reference, however, can be made but by those persons connected with the business of the respective stock offices, and all references are registered, being signed for by the parties making them. The books in this library contain a very interesting and valuable collection of autographs, embracing among their number those of some of the most remarkable persons of their day. The number of books in the Stock Office Library in July, 1888, was: ledgers and alphabets, 4,200; transfer books, 27,675; dividend books, 20,642; powers of attorney, 10,210; odd books, 4,280—total, 67,007.

To carry out the management of the national debt about 175 persons are employed, with an additional staff of about 30, when dividends are paid. Ten rooms are entirely devoted to the purpose, and upwards of 1,700 books are in constant use. The remuneration made to the bank for this service is regulated by an Act of 1861, and amounts at the present time to something over £210,000 per annum. Formerly, the compensation to the bank for managing the national debt was at the rate of £450 per million, but it is now only £300 per million. From the elaborate character of the offices and arrangements, it will be readily understood that the cost of this department is very great, and it is thought the net profit is not more than one-third of the amount received.

There is involved, in the course of each year, the payment, twice over, on 178,000 accounts, of the interest on nearly £630,000,000 of money. In no other country of the civilized world is there exhibited so bright an example of national integrity on the one hand, and of simple, unsuspecting confidence on the other, as is shown in this vast monetary connection betwixt the government and the people.

REGISTER OFFICE—Another office immediately connected with the management of the national debt is the Register Office. In this office a registration is made of all wills and administrations exhibited at the bank, for the purpose of substantiating claims to the various amounts of stock standing in the names of persons deceased. On the following day they are delivered up to the parties depositing the same, or to their order; and, in the meantime, the deceased person's account will have been "made dead," as it is called, in the bank books, in the various stock accounts in which his name may appear. In this way, upwards of 5,000 wills and administrations are dealt with annually.

POST WARRANT OFFICE—The work in this office varies considerably, being especially heavy at the four quarterly periods of the year, when the permanent staff of the office requires to be largely supplemented by extra hands to assist in making out the lists and post the warrants. In the year 1886-7, as many as 131,783 warrants were thus sent.

It is not intended to give here a list of all the stocks which are registered, and the interest on which is payable at the Bank of England. The mode of dealing with all stocks is, as near as circumstances will admit, similar to that adopted in the case of the national debt. The facilities given are equal to, if not in excess of, what could be afforded by any other establishment, and the system is such that every transaction can be referred to with the least possible delay.

NAMES OF THE
GOVERNORS OF THE BANK OF ENGLAND

From its foundation in 1694 to A. D. 1888.

1694-95-96. SIR JOHN HOUBLON.
1697-1698. SIR WILLIAM SCAWEN.
1699-1700. NATHANIEL TENCH.
1701-1702. JOHN WARD.
1703-1704. ABRAHAM HOUBLON.
1705-1706. SIR JAMES BATEMAN.
1707-1708. FRANCIS EYLES.
1709-1710. SIR GILBERT HEATHCOTE.
1711-1712. NATHANIEL GOULD.
1713-1714. JOHN RUDGE.

1715-1716. SIR PETER DELME.
1717-1718. SIR GERARD CONYERS.
1719-1720. JOHN HANGER.
1721-1722. SIR THOMAS SCAWEN.
1723-1724. SIR GILBERT HEATHCOTE.
1725-1726. WILLIAM THOMPSON.
1727-1728. HUMPHRY MORICE.
1729-1730. SAMUEL HOLDEN.
1731-1732. SIR EDWARD BELLAMY.
1733-1734. THE HON. HORATIO TOWNSEND.
1735-1736. BRYAN BENSON.
1737-38-39. THOMAS COOKE.
1740. DELILLERS CARBONNEL.
1741-1742. STAMP BROOKSBANK.
1743-1744. WILLIAM FAWKENER.
1745-1746. CHARLES SAVAGE.
1747-1748. BENJAMIN LONGUST.
1749-50-51. WILLIAN HUNT.
1752-1753. ALEXANDER SHEAFE.
1754-1755. CHARLES PALMER.
1756-1757. MATTHEWS BEACHCROFT.
1758-1759. MERRIK BURRELL.
1760-1761. BARTHOLOMEW BURTON.
1762-1763. ROBERT MARSH.
1764-1765. JOHN WEYLAND.
1766-67-68. MATTHEW CLARMONT.
1769-1770. WILLIAM COOPER.
1771-1772. EDWARD PAYNE.
1773-1774. JAMES SPERLING.
1775-1776. SAMUEL BEACHCROFT.
1777-1778. PETER GAUSSEN.
1779-1780. DANIEL BOOTH.

1781-1782. WILLIAM EWER.
1783-1784. RICHARD NEAVE.
1785-1786. GEORGE PETERS.
1787-1788. EDWARD DARELL.
1789-1790. MARK WEYLAND.
1791-1792. SAMUEL BOSANQUET.
1793-1794. GODFREY THORNTON.
1795-1796. DANIEL GILES.
1797-1798. THOMAS RAIKES.
1799-1800. SAMUEL THORNTON.
1801-1802. JOB MATHEW.
1803. JOSEPH NUTT.
1804-1805. BENJAMIN WINTHROP.
1806-1807. BEESTON LONG.
1808-1809. JOHN WHITMORE.
1810-1811. JOHN PEARSE.
1812-1813. WILLIAM MANNING.
1814-1815. WILLIAM MELLISH.
1816-1817. JEREMIAH HARMAN.
1818-1819. GEORGE DORRIEN.
1820-1821. CHARLES POLE.
1822-1823. JOHN BOWDEN.
1824-1825. CORNELIUS BULLER.
1826-1827. JOHN BAKER RICHARDS.
1828-1829. SAMUEL DREWE.
1830-31-32. JOHN HORSLEY PALMER.
1833-1834. RICHARD MEE RAIKES.
1835-1836. JAMES PATTISON.
1837-1838. TIMOTHY ABRAHAM CURTIS.
1839-1840. SIR JOHN RAE REID, BART.
1841. SIR JOHN HENRY PELLY, BART.
1842-43-44. WILLIAM COTTON.

1845-1846. JOHN BENJAMIN HEATH.
1847. WILLIAM R. ROBINSON.
1847-1848. JAMES MORRIS.
1849-1850. HENRY JAMES PRESCOTT.
1851-1852. THOMSON HANKEY, JR.
1853-1854. JOHN GELLIBRAND HUBBARD.
1855-1856. THOMAS MATTHIAS WEGUELIN.
1857-1858. SHEFFIELD NEAVE.
1859-1860. BONAMY DOBREE.
1861-1862. ALFRED LATHAM.
1863-1864. KIRKMAN DANIEL HODGSON.
1865-1866. HENRY LANCELOT HOLLAND.
1867-1868. THOMAS NEWMAN HUNT.
1869-1870. ROBERT WIGRAM CRAWFORD.
1871-1872. GEORGE LYALL.
1873-1874. BENJAMIN BUCK GREENE.
1875-1876. HENRY HUCKS GIBBS.
1877-1878. EDWARD HOWLEY PALMER.
1879-1880. JOHN WILLIAM BIRCH.
1881-1882. HENRY RIVERSDALE GRENFELL.
1883-1884. JOHN SAUNDERS GILLIAT.
1885-1886. JAMES PATTISON CURRIE.
1887-1888. MARK WILKS COLLET.

CHAPTER XIII.

INTERNAL WORKINGS OF THE BANK OF ENGLAND.

Private Drawing Office—Public Drawing Office—What is Considered a Remunerative Balance—Working Accounts — Number of Bills Issued—Business in the Bill Office—Branch Banks, and How Conducted—Drawing Accounts and Discount Accounts—Important Service Performed by Branch Banks—Number and Location—Rules and Regulations Under Which Accounts are Received in the Bank of England—Denomination of Bank of England Notes.

THE Private Drawing Office is devoted entirely to the management of private accounts. Any person desiring to open a drawing account at the Bank of England, must be respectably introduced to the chief cashier, the sole condition being that the account shall be remunerative to the bank. This condition will be fulfilled if the ordinary balance on the account be sufficient to enable the bank, by the use of such balance at the average rate of interest for money, to realize a profit over and above the expense of keeping the account. The amount of balance required in order that an account may be considered remunerative, will, of course, depend upon the number of cheques paid, and the amount of work otherwise required to be done. There is no stipulated sum insisted upon as a cash balance; but the head of the office will always explain to any person, on his opening an account, what kind of balance would be deemed remunerative. As a rough guess, it has been considered that unless the bank can receive as interest, during the year, 6*d.* for every entry of a cheque paid, there would be no adequate remuneration.

Suppose, for instance, that a customer keeps an average balance of £500, it would be necessary to keep £100 unemployed, and the remaining £400, at 3 per cent., would yield an interest of £12 a year. Now, if not more than 480 cheques are drawn in the year, the balance would be considered remunerative, 480 at 6*d.* being £12. If, however, such account were used at the rate of 1,000 cheques, or drafts for payment, in the course of the year, the case would be different. A few accounts are allowed to be kept without the necessity of a balance being insisted upon; but a charge, in proportion to the quantity of work required to be done, is made annually—this plan is, however, an exception to the general rule.

The bank affords every convenience to its customers, and will buy, or sell, or take charge of securities, receive their dividends of all kinds, and make payments at almost any place; and although accounts are not allowed to be overdrawn, the bank is always ready to discount bills, if considered good, for its customers, and to make advances on such securities as it is in the habit of receiving; but these advantages are only afforded to those who keep either their sole account at the bank, or what is considered a remunerative balance. It is the duty of the head of the office to see that all the accounts are fairly worked, and that the bank is thus remunerated for the work done. If an account is not considered to be fairly worked, the customer is communicated with, and if the representations made are not attended to, the account is ordered to be closed.

The bank, through the Private Drawing Office, grants bills due at seven days' or sixty days' date, the value being paid in cash when the bills are taken out, and the bank becoming responsible for the payment of the bills at maturity. These bills, which can be taken out for uneven amounts, are a great convenience to persons having occasion to remit money to various parts of England, or even foreign countries, as they are readily taken all over the world upon the credit of the Bank of England; and the person wishing to make a remittance knows that the only expense is the loss of the interest on the money. There is generally an outstanding balance of about £170,000, which the bank may make use of; the interest which can be made, minus the expense of the office and printing the bills, being to the profit of the bank. There are about 40,000 bills issued in the course of the year in London and at the branches, representing an aggregate of about £5,000,000. All the money collected throughout the country by the revenue officers for customs and excise dues, taxes, etc., are paid into it, and all payments on account of the public service are made by orders made on it.

The separation of the public from the private accounts is merely made to insure, by the subdivision of labor, greater convenience, both to the public generally and to the clerks of the bank. There is no practical difference whether money is paid or received on a government account, or on any other account which may be kept at this separate department; all receipts in the day go to the credit of deposits, and all payments are charged to deposits, and the balance at the close of the day must agree with the cash brought in to the cashiers as money not used, after accounting for all payments and receipts made during the day; and the daily business of the bank is not considered as concluded until the balance is found correct.

In the Bill Office all bills of exchange belonging to customers, or bills which have been discounted and belong to the bank, are kept duly sorted and so arranged as to be presented without fail at maturity. All cheques paid into the Private and Public Drawing Offices, and all cheques received from the country, are sent to this office for collection, and the proceeds passed to the credit of their respective owners. Cheques and bills on clearing bankers are collected through the clearing house; those on non-clearing bankers, merchants and others, through the out-tellers' department. There is a collection for the latter class at eleven o'clock in the forenoon for cheques, etc., paid to account in the Drawing Offices the previous day, and another collection at one o'clock for those paid in on the same day. Cheques and bills on clearing bankers are sent to the clearing house, the last charge being made up to 3.45 o'clock. All cheques paid in up to that hour may be drawn against the same day.

Although this office adds nothing to the revenues of the bank, it is most important in the economy of the general business, performing, as it does, the part of collecting agent for the other departments, in presenting, under a system which insures unerring precision and great promptitude, all the cheques, etc., which they have received, and all bills or interest notes which are payable at a distant date.

If cheques requiring collection at a distance are paid in to the credit of an account, time must be allowed for the receipt of money before it can be drawn against; but the endeavor of the Bank of England is to afford every facility consistent with security to enable its customers to make use of every kind of order for payment, by turning it into cash as quickly as practicable. In the Private Drawing Office there are about 112 clerks employed, and nearly 200 books are in constant use.

The Public Drawing Office, as its name implies, is devoted to the custody of the drawing accounts of the government and various public companies and institutions, although there is, of course, practically no difference between the accounts of the government and those of the private customers of the bank.

When branch banks of the Bank of England were first broached they were not viewed with favor by country bankers, who saw that their profits and influence would be depreciated. Since 1826, the bank has established branches in some of the great commercial towns. Following will be found the mode of conduct of business, which is about the same as the parent bank :—

For instance, the branch at Liverpool, and the same is true of those established in other places, is to be a secure place of deposit for persons having occasion to make use of a bank for that purpose. Such persons are said to have *drawing accounts*. To facilitate to the mercantile and trading classes the obtaining discounts of good and unexceptionable bills, founded upon real transactions, two approved names are required upon every bill or note discounted. These are called *discount accounts*. The applications of parties who desire to open discount accounts at the branch are forwarded to the parent bank in London for approval. When approved, good bills may be discounted at branches without further reference to London. Bills payable at London, or any place where a branch is established, are discounted under this regulation. The dividends on any of the public funds, which are payable at the Bank of England, may be received at any branch by persons who have opened drawing accounts, after signing powers of attorney for that purpose, which the branch will procure from London. No charge is made in this case, except the expense of the power of attorney and the postage incurred in transmitting it. Purchases and sales of every description of government securities are effected by the branch at a charge corresponding to that made by the local bankers where the branch is situated. A commission, including brokerage in London, and all expenses of postage, is charged on paying at the Bank of England bills accepted by persons having drawing accounts at branches. All branches grant bills on London, payable at seven days' date, without acceptance, for sums of £10 and upward. Persons having a drawing account at a branch may order money to be paid at the bank in London to their credit at the branch and *vice versa*. Bank post bills, which are accepted and due, are received at the branch from parties having drawing accounts. No interest is allowed on deposits. No advance is made by a branch upon any description of landed or other property, nor is any account allowed to be overdrawn. The notes are the same as those issued by the parent establishment, except being dated at the branch, and made payable there and in London.

There are two branches in London and nine in the country. Those in London are the Western Branch and the Law Courts Branch. They do not issue notes, but carry on only just such banking business as is carried on by other banks in the same districts. The country branches, naming them in order of their importance, are: Liverpool, Manchester, Newcastle-on-Tyne, Leeds, Birmingham, Hull, Bristol, Plymouth, Portsmouth. These all carry on ordinary banking business, but do not compete for it very keenly. Their business mainly lies in the issue of notes, and in affording convenience for the collection of the revenue, and for the disbursements of some of the large government establishments. The notes issued by each branch are payable in cash only at that branch, and notes issued by the head office are, likewise, payable there only.

The branches of the Bank of England, both in London and in the country, each of which is under the charge of an agent and sub-agent, are all perfectly subordinate to the parent establishment. They carry on all the ordinary business of local banking, such as receiving deposits payable on demand, transmitting money, receiving money for customers at all places, and taking charge of securities; in short, each branch carries on the same kind of business as is conducted in the drawing (or ordinary banking) offices in London in addition to the issue of bank notes (so far as the country branches are concerned), seven days' bills, or bills at longer dates. The notes issued at a particular branch are payable in cash only at that branch, or in London; and it should be borne in mind that bank notes issued by the head office are not payable in cash on demand at any of the branches, whether in London or the country. The accounts are balanced every night, exactly as in London, and the balance sent up to London daily by post, together with particulars of all the transactions of each day. Any sum of money may be remitted from London to any branch, or between the respective branches, where also stockholders can now have their dividends paid. There are nine of these country branches, and about one hundred and fifty persons are employed at them. One of the most important services performed through the branch banks is the remittance of the revenue, which is paid over by the collectors at the various places of receipt to clerks attending from the branch banks for the purpose. Credit is then immediately given to the exchequer account in London, so that the revenue is made available for the public service with the least possible loss of time.

Following are the rules and regulations for the general conduct of the business of the Bank of England:—

1. All letters should be addressed to the chief cashier.

2. It is desirable that drafts should be drawn upon cheques furnished by the bank.

3. Cheques upon city bankers, eastward of King street, Cheapside,—

Paid in by 12 o'clock may be drawn for after 1.
Do.   2 o'clock   "   "   after 3.

4. Cheques paid in after 2, and before 3 o'clock, and cheques upon all other London bankers paid in before 12 o'clock, may be drawn for on the following morning.

5. Cheques paid in after 3 o'clock are sent out at 9 the following morning, and may be drawn for as soon as received.

6. Dividend warrants are received at the drawing office until 4 o'clock in the afternoon for all persons having accounts at the bank.

7. It is requested that notice be given at the drawing office of bills accepted payable at the bank, with the date of their maturity.

8. Persons keeping a drawing account with the bank (although not having a discount account) may tender bills for discount through the drawing office. Application for discounts or for advances on stock, exchequer bills, &c., must be made before 2 o'clock.

9. Bills of exchange and notes not paid when due will be noted.

10. The bank will make purchases or sales of British or foreign securities upon an order in writing addressed to the chief cashier; and dividends on stock may be received under powers of attorney granted to the cashiers of the bank.

11. Exchequer bills, bonds, railway debentures, or any other securities may be deposited, and the interest, when payable, will be received and placed to account.

12. Credits paid in to account are received without the bank-book, and are afterwards entered therein without the party claiming them.

13. Notes of country bankers, payable in London, are sent out the same day for payment if paid in before 3 o'clock.

14. The pass-books should be left at the drawing office, at least once a month, to be written up.

15. Where post-bills are required, or a payment is to be made to any office of the bank by cheque on the Bank of England, the cheque must be presented at the office upon which it is drawn, and exchanged for an order on the post-bill office, or on the office at which the payment is to be made.

16. Cash-boxes taken in, contents unknown, for such parties as keep accounts at the bank.

17. A person having a drawing account may have a discount account; but no person can have the latter without at the same time having the former. When a discount account is opened, the signatures of the parties are entered in a book kept for that purpose, and powers of attorney are granted empowering the persons named in them to act for their principals. Bills of exchange having more than 95 days to run are not eligible for discount.

N. B.—All changes in the residence of persons keeping cash at the bank are requested to be made known at the drawing office; and it is particularly requested that no gratuities be offered to the clerks of the banking offices, such gratuities being strictly forbidden.

The denominations of Bank of England notes are £5, £10, £20, £30, £50, £100, £200, £300, £500, £1,000. No notes are issued of less than £5. During the years from 1797 to 1821, the bank issued notes for £1 and £2, but they ceased issuing them in the latter year, and paid them off in 1822.

CHAPTER XIV.

BUSINESS OF THE BANKING DEPARTMENT.

How it is Conducted—Amounts Cheques may be Drawn for—Opening an Account with the Bank—Business the Bank Transacts for Customers—Bank Deposits—Profits of the Bank—How Derived—Expenses of the Bank—Weekly Bank Statement Given and Analyzed—Proportion of Assets to Liabilities.

THE business of the Banking Department—which, except as regards the magnitude of its transactions, and the current accounts of other bankers and of the government, differs but little from that of any other London or American bank—is carried on chiefly in the Private Drawing Office, the Public Drawing Office, the Discount Office and the Bill and Post Bill Offices. Besides these offices, there are the Dividend Pay Office, devoted to the cash payment of dividends, and the chief cashier's office, where advances on securities and the various public loans are initiated, and to which is attached the private room of the chief cashier, which, for the most part, corresponds with the manager's room in any ordinary bank.

Formerly, the business transacted at the Bank of England was so much encumbered with forms and conditions, that the generality of merchants and ordinary people rarely thought of employing it to keep their money or make their payments. But in this respect an entire change has been effected. Cheques, the minimum amount of which was formerly £10, may now be drawn for any amount, great or small; and all sorts of banking business is conducted with facility and dispatch, and, it may be added, with perfect security.

The bank opens banking accounts, or, as they are called, "drawing accounts," for the safe custody, and the receipt and payment of cash, not only with merchants and traders, but with all persons who choose to keep their money at a banker's and draw cheques against it. The bank also takes charge of its customer's bills of exchange, the exchange of exchequer bills, the receipt of dividends, etc., free of charge. Plate chests, and deed and security boxes, may be deposited free of expense, by customers, for safe custody. The bank looks to the average balance of cash on each account to compensate for the trouble and expense for keeping it, and in this respect the requirements of the bank are certainly not greater than those of ordinary bankers. No particular sum is to be lodged on opening an account, it is only necessary that the party should be known as respectable, and in a condition to require a banking account. But the bank receives and holds sums of money for safe custody for parties who have no current accounts.

The bank affords every convenience to its customers, and buys or sells or takes care of securities, receives dividends of all kinds, and makes payments anywhere required. Although the accounts are not allowed to be overdrawn, it is always ready to discount satisfactory bills for its customers, and to make advances on a certain class of securities. In brief, it is what all other banks are, and this part of its business is conducted on substantially the same basis as theirs, with perhaps a little more caution and exclusiveness.

It is not necessary to enter at length on the subject of the general management of the bank, as the principle on which business is carried on does not differ from any other well-conducted bank. The average amount of deposits being known, and due regard paid to the temporary or permanent character of the same, the first duty of every banker is to invest, in the best banking securities, all above the amount to which such deposits are likely to be reduced.

When it is considered that the total deposits in the Bank of England vary from £30,000,000 to £40,000,000, it can readily be imagined that the securities in which these deposits are invested, and the amount kept daily in reserve, form a very important part of the duty devolving on the directors, and especially on the governors, who have all such accounts and charges under their direct observation.

The principal item in the private deposits is the total of the balances of the other London bankers. From 1845 to 1877, a return was made showing the amount of the banker's balances, but since the latter date this information has not been given. In 1845 and 1846, the totals of these balances averaged respectively £1,250,000 and £1,400,000, whilst in 1877 they averaged £9,500,000. It is by means of this office that the London bankers make all their settlements between one another. The non-clearing bankers pay all charges presented by bankers by means of drafts on a clearing banker or upon the Bank of England. The clearing bankers settle their differences at the clearing house by means of transfers from their own accounts to that of the clearing house, or *vice versa*, the clearing house having also an account at the bank, and, of course, the transactions therein balance every day, with the exception of the trifling difference running on for errors in the settlement.

The total of deposits, both public and private, held by the Bank of England at its head office and its branches, on 15th of August, 1888, was £27,777,836. This was somewhat below the usual figure. In the ten years, 1876-1885, the deposits averaged more than £31,000,000.

As to the profits earned by the Bank of England, there have on many occasions been reports made to parliament giving particulars of the principal sources of profit, but some of these have been materially reduced during recent years. In the first place, the charge for managing the National Debt is £300 per million. The management of the entire public debt of Great Britain is placed in the hands of the Bank of England. Then again the profits on the note issue is considerable. The bank also has the profits to be derived from the use of its deposits. There is generally an average of about £20,000,000 to be employed in various ways. There is also the profit on the buying and selling of gold in the bullion department, which is stated as bringing in from £25,000 to £45,000 per annum. There is also the interest receivable on the investment of the large capital, £14,553,000. Of this,

£11,015,100 is lent to the government, and bears, at present, 3 per cent. interest. The remainder is invested in miscellaneous British securities. There is also a profit derived from the agencies. The estimated net profits of the bank are about £1,450,000 per annum.

Although the profits are large, there are deductions to be made. The bank has to pay to the government £60,000 per annum for the stamp duty on its notes, and a fixed sum of £120,000 out of the profits, besides the whole profit on the £2,200,000 extra issue against securities. In 1886, the bank paid to the government under these three heads £213,895, being more than £20,000 over the amount received for the management of the national debt. No account is ever rendered of the profits or expenses of the bank for public perusal.

The "Banking Department" of the Bank of England is the separation of the ordinary banking business from the business of financial agency and issuing notes.

The Bank Act of 1844 does not touch the management of the Banking Department in any way beyond requiring that a weekly statement of its assets and liabilities shall be published. A specimen statement is given following this paragraph. This statement—which forms part of the "Bank Return"—may be thus analyzed. On one side are the liabilities, divided into the liability towards the proprietors of the bank, as shown by the amounts of "Proprietors' Capital" and "Rest" (which latter is practically an addition to the capital); the liability to the government, as shown by the amount of "Public Deposits," which are the balances of different government accounts; the liability to the customers, as shown by the amount of the "Other Deposits," which are the sum of the balances of the current or "drawing" accounts and the liability to the holders of the bank's acceptances, as shown by the amount of "Seven-day and other Bills" in circulation. On the other side of the statement are the assets by which these liabilities are represented, divided into "Government Securities," which show the amount of the banking capital invested in government securities; the "Other Securities," which show the amount of other investments made by the bank; and, separately, the "notes" and "gold and silver coin," which show the amount of cash in hand for the current purposes of the Banking Department. This sum of notes and gold and silver coin forms, so to speak, the cash assets of the bank, and the proportion which it bears to the current liabilities disclosed by the public and other deposits and seven-day bills is called the proportion of reserve to liabilities, and is always a matter of great interest, and often of great anxiety, to London on Thursdays, the day on which the "Bank Return" is issued.

The question of the proportion which these cash assets should bear to liabilities is one of extreme importance to a prudent banker. It is generally considered that it should be about one-third. The publication of the weekly bank return is useful and important to commerce, banking and finance. The Bank of England, through its banking department, undertakes duties merely towards its own customers and the government. Its banking business is conducted for the most part (in theory, at all events,) on the same lines as any other banking institution.

BANK OF ENGLAND STATEMENT.

Following is a specimen of the weekly bank statement issued in conformity with the Act of Parliament of 1844, viz. :—

An account pursuant to the Act 7 and 8 Vict. cap. 32, for the week ending on Wednesday, August 22, 1888.

Issue Department.

Notes Issued..........	£35,164,220	Government Debt.....	£11,015,100
		Other Securities.......	5,184,900
		Gold Coin and Bullion.	18,964,220
		Silver Bullion.........	—
	£35,164,220		£35,164,220

Dated the 21st day of August, 1888.

F. MAY, Chief Cashier.

Banking Department.

Proprietors' Capital....	£14,553,000	Government Securities.	£15,017,396
Rest	3,390,734	Other Securities.......	18,433,287
Public Deposits (including Exchequer, Savings Banks, Commissioners of Nat'l. Debt, & Dividend Accounts)	3,143,939	Notes	10,587,105
		Gold and Silver Coin...	1,340,287
Other Deposits.........	24,118,044		
7 Day and other Bills. .	172,358		
	£45,378,075		£45,378,075

Dated the 21st day of August, 1888.

F. MAY, Chief Cashier.

The prominent feature in the return is the separation of the business of the bank into the two distinct departments, dealing respectively with Issue and Banking.

CHAPTER XV.

DISCOUNTS, DIVIDENDS, LOANS AND RULES.

Duties of the Discount Office—Precaution Before Discounting — Powers of the Directors — Who Are Allowed Discount Accounts—Checking a Speculative Tendency—Inconsistency of Long Date Discounts—Opinion of an English Writer—Real and Fictitious Transactions—Rules to Observe—Who Controls the Rate of Discount?— False Notions Regarding the Power of the Bank of England—Rate of Discount from 1794 to Date—Dividends on Bank of England Stock from 1694 to 1888—The Price of Bank Stock and How Bought and Sold.

The Discount Office is charged with the reception of all bills offered for discount by parties who have opened discount accounts with the bank. These bills are submitted to a committee of directors (sitting daily for the purpose) who decide upon the amount of accommodation to be granted and the rate of discount to be charged. The net proceeds of the bills discounted are then passed to the credit of the customer's account, while the bills themselves are entrusted to the care of the Bill Office, which occupies itself with the duty of sorting and arranging them so that they may be duly presented for payment at maturity.

The bank employs a certain amount of its usual deposits in discounting, as it is considered one of the very best modes in which money payable on demand can be safely used. If the sum so employed were generally kept up to about the same proportion of the deposits, say one-third or one-half, the utmost limit of the date at which bills become due, commonly called the *echeance*, being ninety days, and the average about sixty-eight days, the amount returning to the bank for bills daily falling due would be about the same; and thus a very satisfactory control over these resources of the bank would be maintained. But this state of things, owing to the ordinary habits of London, and the great dependence placed on the Bank of England to supply additional funds at periods when money or capital has become unduly engaged, it is extremely difficult to maintain; and, consequently, in the management of this description of security the greatest care is required. It has been held by some authorities that the power of raising the rate of interest to an unlimited extent is sufficient to protect the Bank of England against an undue amount of pressure; but, practically, this has not been exercised with much severity. It has very frequently occurred that, after a long succession of very low rates of interest, indicating a great abundance of unemployed capital, an extent of business has been undertaken far beyond what a judicious regard to safety should have induced; and if, when this state of things is in existence, any sudden apprehension of an approaching scarcity of capital should occur, no rise in the rate of discount at the bank will immediately check the demand; on the contrary, for a certain time the very opposite effect may be produced, and it is, therefore, very necessary for the Bank of England to have other sources on which it may depend for a supply of money on such occasions.

But the prevalent desire to extend discount operations, especially by those banking establishments who make their money principally by the difference between the interest allowed on deposits, and that which they can make by employment of the same, renders it quite impossible for the bank, however prudently its own business may have been managed, to make others, with whose conduct it has nothing whatever to do, equally circumspect. At particular periods, for many years past, it has invariably been found that the Bank of England has been looked to for an unusual supply of money, at the very time when other banking establishments, and especially the bill brokers of London, have had less available money at their command than usual.

Any person who is carrying on a respectable business in London can have a discount account at the Bank of England, if introduced by any director to whom he may be known, or by introduction to the governors with such references as they may think fit to require; and when once introduced and a discount account opened, he may send in bills daily for discount, the quality of the bills, and the amount to be granted, being subject to the approval of the directors in daily attendance.

The Bank of England rarely discounts bills that have more than two, or at most three months to run. The discounting of bills at long dates is a powerful stimulus to unsafe speculation. When individuals obtain loans which they are not to be called upon to pay for six, twelve, or, perhaps, eighteen months, they are tempted to adventure in speculations which are not expected to be wound up till some proportionately distant period; and as these not unfrequently fail, the consequence is that, when the bills become due, there is commonly little or no provision made for their payment. In such cases, the discounters, to avert an imminent loss, sometimes consent to renew the bills. But, while a proceeding of this sort is rarely productive of ultimate advantage to either party, the fact of its having taken place makes other adventurers reckon that, in the event of their speculations proving to be less successful than they anticipated, their bills will be treated in the same manner, and thus aggravates and extends the evil.

In other respects, too, the discounting of bills at long dates, or their renewal, or the making of permanent loans, is altogether inconsistent with sound banking principles, for it prevents the bankers from having that command over their resources which is advantageous at all times, and indispensable in periods of difficulty or distress.

In the discounting of bills, a great deal of stress is usually laid, or pretended to be laid, on the distinction between those that arise out of real transactions and those that are fictitious or that are intended for accommodation purposes. The former are said to be legitimate, while the latter are stigmatized as illegitimate. Mr. Thornton, in his work on the Paper-Credit of Great Britain, has shown that the difference is neither so well marked nor so wide as many suppose. A notion seems to be generally entertained that all real bills are drawn against produce of one sort or other, which (or its value) is supposed to form a fund for their payment. Such, however, is not always, nor even most commonly, the case.

A, for example, sells to B certain produce, for which he draws a bill at sixty days' date. But prices are rising, trade is brisk, or a spirit of speculation is afloat, and, in a week or two (sometimes much less), B sells the produce at an advance to C, who thereafter sells it to D, and so on. Hence it may, and, in fact, frequently does happen, that bills amounting to four, five, or even ten times the value of a quantity of merchandise, have grown out of its successive sales, before the first of the series has become due. And not only this, but bills are themselves very frequently rediscounted; and in this case the credit of the last indorser is generally the only thing looked to; and there is not, perhaps, one case in ten in which any inquiries are made in regard to the origin and history of the bills, though they are often of the most questionable description.

On the whole, therefore, it would seem that the real or presumed solvency of the parties signing a bill, and responsible for its payment, is the only safe criterion by which to judge whether it should or should not be discounted. But the fact of a merchant or other trader offering accommodation bills for discount ought unquestionably to excite a suspicion that he is trading beyond his capital.

A writer in an English magazine says:—

" Besides bills avowedly intended for accommodation

purposes, another and a different variety of such bills is drawn by parties at a distance from each other, often men of straw, and made to appear as if they were bottomed on real transactions. Bills of this sort are, it is greatly to be regretted, always current, and often to a large extent. Of course no person of respectability can be knowingly connected with such bills, which are almost always put in motion either to bolster up some bankrupt concern, or to cheat and defraud the public. But despite the mischief of which they are productive, it appears to be pretty generally supposed that the currency of these bills is an evil which cannot be prevented. There can, however, be no real doubt that it may, at all events, be very greatly diminished; and this desirable result would be effected were it enacted that all bills shall henceforth bear upon their face what they really are; that those that are intended for accommodation purposes shall have at their head the words "*Accommodation bill;*" and that those only shall bear to be for "value received" that have grown out of *bona fide* transfers of property. An enactment of this sort could not be felt as a grievance by anyone unless he had a fraudulent purpose in view. And were the impressing of a false character on a bill made a criminal offence, punishable by several years' imprisonment, there is every probability that a formidable check would be given to the issue of spurious bills, and to the manifold abuses to which the practice gives rise."

Bill discounters, who have got fictitious paper on their hands, and attempt to get rid of it by concealing its character or representing it in a favorable light, make themselves parties to the fraud. Such conduct is so very flagitious, that when it can be fairly brought home to the parties, it should subject them to the severest penalties.

The Bank of England is so large a holder of money that to some extent it controls the rate of discount; the discount it demands determines all other banks in fixing their rate. Many persons believe, the late Walter Bagehot has written, that the Bank of England has some peculiar power of fixing the value of money.

Mr. Bagehot further says:—"They see that the bank varies its minimum rate of discount from time to time, and that, more or less, all other banks follow its lead, and charge as much as it charges, and they are puzzled why this should be. The explanation is simple. The value of money is settled by the law of supply and demand, as that of all other commodities is. The Bank of England used to be the predominant, and is still a most important, dealer in money. It states the lowest price at which it will dispose of its stock of money, and its quotation enables other dealers to obtain that price, or something near it. The reason is obvious. At all ordinary moments there is not enough money in the market unless some is taken from the Bank of England. As soon as the bank rate of interest is fixed, a great many persons who have bills to discount try to see how much cheaper than at that rate they can get them done for. They seldom can get them done for much less than the bank would charge, for if they did every one would leave the bank, and the outer market would have more bills than it could bear. Should the bank see this beginning, it would lower its rate, so as to secure a reasonable portion of the business to itself."

The notion that the Bank of England has absolute

control over the money market, and can fix the rate of discount as it likes, has survived, continues Mr. Bagehot, from the days before 1844, when it could issue as many notes as it liked, and even then the notion was a mistake.

In order to understand the action of the Bank of England correctly, it must always be borne in mind that, since the Act of 1844, the directors have had no control over that part of the currency which consists of bank notes; that is, they have had nothing whatever to do with the amount at any time in circulation in the country. The only function of the bank in this respect is to give notes for sovereigns, when the latter exceed five in number, or for bar gold, and to give or return sovereigns for every bank note presented for payment.

The rates of discount charged by the bank since its establishment are as follows:

	Per cent.
From Aug. 8, 1694, to Aug. 30, 1694, on foreign bills	6
Aug. 30, 1694, to Jan. 16, 1695, on foreign bills	4½
Oct. 24, 1694, to Jan. 16, 1695, on inland bills	6
Jan. 16, 1695, to May 19, 1695, on foreign bills	6
Jan. 16, 1695, to May 19, 1695, to customers of the bank	3
Jan. 16, 1695, to July 26, 1716, on inland bills	4½
May 19, 1695, to Feb. 28, 1704, on foreign bills	4
May 19, 1695, to Feb. 28, 1704, on foreign bills not payable at the bank	5
Feb. 28, 1704, to June 22, 1710, on foreign bills	5
June 22, 1710, to July 26, 1716, on foreign and inland bills	4
July 26, 1716, to April 30, 1719, on bills and notes	5

Oct. 27, 1720, to Aug. 23, 1722, on bills.......	4
Aug. 23, 1722, to Oct. 18, 1742, on inland bills	5
Aug. 23, 1722, to Oct. 18, 1742, on foreign bills	4
Oct. 18, 1742, to Dec. 12, 1744, on foreign bills	5
Dec. 12, 1744, to May 1, 1746, on foreign bills (15 days to run)......................	4
Dec. 12, 1744, to May 1, 1746, on inland bills..	5
May 1, 1746, to June 20, 1822, on bills and notes (95 days to run)..................	4
June 20, 1822, to Dec. 13, 1825, on bills and notes (95 days to run)..................	5
Dec. 13, 1825, to July 5, 1827, on bills and notes (95 days to run)..................	5
July 5, 1827, to July 21, 1836, on bills and notes (95 days to run)..................	4
July 21, 1836, to Sept. 1, 1836, on bills and notes (95 days to run)..................	4½
Feb. 13, 1838, to May 16, 1839, on bills and notes (95 days to run)..................	4
May 16, 1839, to June 20, 1839, on bill and notes (95 days to run)..................	5
Aug. 1, 1839, to Jan. 23, 1840, on bills and notes (95 days to run)..................	6
Jan. 23, 1840, to Oct. 15, 1840, on 65-day bills.	5
Oct. 15, 1840, to June 3, 1841, on 95-day bills.	5
June 3, 1841, to April 7, 1842, on 95-day bills.	5
April 7, 1842, to Sept. 5, 1844, on 95-day bills.	4
Sept. 5, 1844, to March 13, 1845, on bills......	2½
Sept. 5, 1844, to March 13, 1845, on notes.....	3

Since 1845, the changes have been more numerous. In 1847, there were 10 changes; in 1861, 13; 1864, 14;

1873, 14; 1879, 13; 1884, 10; and so on, with hundreds of fluctuations to date. We give above the rate for many different years, which is enough to show the frequency of changes and uncertainty in the rates of discounts.

The dividends on bank stock of the Bank of England from the establishment, in 1694, to the present time, 1888, have been as follows:—

Years.	Dividend.	Years.	Dividend.
1694.	8 per cent.	1865.	11¼ per cent.
1697.	9 "	1866.	10¼ "
1708.	Varied from 9 to	1867.	10 "
1729.	5½ per cent.	1868.	8 "
1730.	6 "	1869.	8¾ "
1731.	5½ "	1872.	9½ "
1721.	6 "	1873.	10 "
1728.	5½ "	1874.	10 "
1747.	5 "	1875.	9 "
1753.	4½ "	1876.	9 "
1764.	5 "	1877.	9½ "
1767.	5½ "	1878.	9½ "
1781.	6 "	1879.	10½ "
1788.	7 "	1880.	9½ "
1807.	10 "	1881.	9½ "
1823.	8 "	1882.	10½ "
1839.	7 "	1883.	10¼ "
1852.	7½ "	1884.	9¾ "
1853.	8 "	1885.	10 "
1856.	9½ "	1886.	9½ "
1859.	8½ "	1887.	9¾ "
1863.	8¾ "	1888.	9½ " Est.
1864.	9¾ "		

The stock is bought and sold upon the market in the same manner as other stocks are dealt in. For many years past the dividend paid has averaged about 9 per cent., and the price of the stock has generally been quoted about 300. Of late it has participated in the general rise in price of first-class securities, and is now quoted at about 325.

CHAPTER XVI.

ENGLISH AND AMERICAN CLEARING HOUSES.

How they Originated in London—Primitive Manner of Conducting Business—How Transacted To-day and Amount of Business Annually Done—A Clearing House for Country Bankers—American Clearing Houses—Detailed Statement of the Routine Business in the New York Clearing House—Scene in the Clearing Room During Business Hours—Specimen Credit Ticket—How the Banks are Represented and Settlements Are Made—The Settling Clerk and the Delivery Clerk—Duties of the Proof Clerk—Specimen Sheet of Clearing House Proof—Penalty for Making Errors—Specimen Sheet of Settling Clerk's Statement.

NOT many years after the London bankers had ceased to issue notes, the inconvenience of making all payments in Bank of England notes and gold had become so great, that some change was indispensably necessary, when the plan of adjusting each other's daily payments by an interchange of liabilities was adopted, as the best mode of economizing the use of money.

At first the system adopted was of the most primitive kind, and certainly not the safest. The clerks of the various banking houses used to perform the operation of exchanges at the corners of streets and on the top of a post; then they met by appointment at a public house; but, from the insecurity of these arrangements it was at last thought best that the principal city bankers should rent a house where all the banks should meet. This house was named the clearing house.

The clearing house in London was established over a century ago. It was first used as a place where the clerks of the bankers in the city of London could assemble daily to exchange with one another the cheques drawn upon and bills payable at their respective houses. The clearing house is an institution founded, not merely upon the idea of saving time and trouble in the use of the precious metals, but also of circulating notes. All the banks and bankers associated as members of a clearing house are for this purpose, as it were, but one individual. The clearing house of London, the first of its kind in the history of finance, originated among the bankers of that city, whose transactions in the cheques, bills, and drafts drawn upon each other became so large as to call for the daily and even hourly use of vast sums in bank notes by all of them. Appreciating how readily the debits and credits respectively due or held by them might be set off, the one against the other, they formed the clearing house, where up to 4 o'clock each day all drafts, bills, etc., drawn upon each individual member were taken. The system of the London clearing house has recently been much extended and improved, and all balances are settled by cheques drawn upon the Bank of England—no bank notes being required at all.

Before the clearing house existed, each banker had to send a clerk to the places of business of all the other bankers in London to collect the sums payable to them in respect of cheques and bills; and it is obvious that much time was consumed by this process, which involved also the use of an unnecessary quantity of money and corresponding risks of safe carriage. In 1775, the common centre of exchange was agreed upon. Its use was confined to the bankers,—at that time and long afterwards exclusively private bankers,—doing business within the city, and the bankers in the west end of the metropolis used some one or other of the city banks as their agent in clearing, a practice which still continues. When the joint-stock banks were first established, the jealousy of the existing banks was powerful enough to exclude them altogether from the use of the clearing house; and some years elapsed before this feeling was removed so as to allow them to be admitted.

At first the clearing house was simply a place of meeting, but it came to be perceived that the sorting and distributing of cheques, bills, &c., could be more expeditiously conducted by the appointment of two or three common clerks to whom each banker's clerk could give all the instruments of exchange he wished to collect, and from whom he could receive all those payable at his own house. The payment of the balance settled the transaction, and an analysis of the statistics of the clearing house, as far back as 1856, shows that the amount of cash that passed was often less than 4 per cent. of the total sums cleared. Latterly, however, the arrangements of the clearing house have been further perfected, so that neither notes nor coin are now required. The clearing house, as well as each banker using it, has an account at the Bank of England; and the balances due at the close of each day's transactions are settled by transfers from one account to another at the bank.

The use of the clearing house was still further extended in 1858, so as to include the settlement of exchanges between the country bankers of England. Before that time each country banker receiving cheques on other country bankers sent them to those other bankers by post (supposing they were not carrying on business in the same place), and requested that the amount should be paid by the London agent of the banker on whom the cheques were drawn to the London agent remitting them. Cheques were thus collected by correspondence, and each remittance involved a separate payment in London. In 1858, it was proposed to set up a country clearing house in London; but it was suggested by Sir John Lubbock that the existing establishment could accomplish what was desired, and this was eventually done. A country banker now sends cheques on other country banks to his London correspondent, who exchanges them at the clearing house with the correspondents of the bankers on whom they are drawn. It will be easily understood that an extraordinary economy in the use of coin has resulted from these arrangements. Statistics have been given, showing that out of the sum of a million dollars paid into a certain bank, only £4,500 was in bank-notes, and £6,210 of coin. In 1868, the weekly average clearance of the London clearing house was about £65,397,075.

In 1873, the average weekly clearance was £116,254,-717. In 1887, the average weekly clearance was £475,-758,000. Total clearance of the London clearing house for 1887 was £6,077,097,000.

The American clearing house is founded upon the English system in general, although the detail work is somewhat different.

The New York clearing house is a building, or rather, nine series of connected rooms in a building, in which each of a certain number of banks daily delivers to every other bank, sustaining associated relations with it, all the bills, drafts, and cheques drawn upon or payable at that bank in the course of the preceding day. It also receives from every other bank all the drafts and cheques drawn upon it, together with all the bills payable by or at it. Sometimes the difference between the sums total is in its favor, in which case it receives through its messenger the balance due. At other times, the difference is against it, and must be promptly liquidated by cash or its authorized representatives. This entire process is designated by the expressive term *clearing*, because it clears off all pecuniary obligations due from, and claims of, all connected fiscal institutions upon each other.

We are indebted to "The Office" for the following description of the New York clearing house: The scene in the clearing room during business hours is a busy and pleasing one. The arrangement of the working room consists in three rows of double desks, each desk numbered, and bearing on a silver plate in front the name of the bank to whose use it is appropriated. Elegant, polished, furnished with seats, drawers, and other conveniences for the clerks, these desks are separated from each other by wire guards, and stretch from one end of the room to the other. Two high wire railings, each with a row of benches, and providing for transit by opening in the middle, separate each line of desks from its neighbor. The design of this arrangement is obvious enough, as the clerks from member banks pour in. Young, middle-aged, and old, sprightly and sedate, dudes and doctors, all on serious thought intent. Their business demands alertness, care, efficiency. Some are settling, others delivery clerks.

Upon entering the room, every settling clerk lays down upon the table a credit ticket, of which a sample is given herewith:—

NEW YORK CLEARING HOUSE.	No. 27.		NEW YORK CLEARING HOUSE,
			November 1st, 1888.
	Debit................................NATIONAL BANK, Amount received $957,853.13		
	Credit...........................	"	brought $2,001,819.27
	$.... ....Debit balance due Clearing-house		
	Credit balance due.............................NATIONAL BANK, $1,043,466.14		
			THOMAS ROGERS,
			Settling Clerk.

SPECIMEN CREDIT TICKET.

This credit ticket shows the amount of exchanges sent by his employers. The settling clerk then seats himself at the compartment bearing the number and name of his bank, while the delivery clerk of the same bank assumes a standing position opposite to him.

Precisely at 10 A. M., two taps of a gong announce everything ready for business. Another tap and the financial procession begins its march. Delivery clerks, exchanges arranged in box or on arm, each deposits a brown manila envelope containing checks, drafts and bills, and with ticket memorandum of amount attached, on the counter of every debtor institution in consecutive order, taking written acknowledgement of receipt on his "Delivery Clerk's Statement," and thus securing vouchers for the due distribution of his exchanges, until the round is completed, and he finds himself exhausted of packages and standing at the point of departure.

In the brief space of ten minutes no less than 4,032 have been effected and receipts therefor given by the settling clerks, who enter upon their settling sheets the amount of exchanges brought by each associated bank opposite its printed name. The Strasburg clock is not more measured or precise in its movements, nor more unfailing in its accuracy, than the living automaton, the New York clearing house. In fifteen minutes all, or nearly all, the delivery clerks have disappeared.

After the delivery clerk has returned to his bank, the settling clerk remains to make proof. Adding up the several items of receipt from the creditor banks, he inscribes the aggregate, with other particulars, upon a debit ticket, which is collected by a junior clerk.

A proof clerk revises everything. He occupies a platform with the manager and the assistant manager. While the proof clerk is revising the reports, the settling clerk is busy on his own private sheet. Exchanges received here have been sent to the bank, but the tickets that accompanied them on presentation at the clearing house have been retained at his desk. By means of these he corrects original entries, if so be that he has fallen into error at the time of reception. In this way the proof of certainty is made manifest. Absolute accuracy is rarely achieved on the first trial. Life is too full of disturbing influences to quietly leave every scrivener in full control of his powers. Thought may dart off to one or more of a hundred objects, instead of fixing itself exclusively on the settling clerk's statement. Five errors are made to-day. Sometimes the number rises to twenty-five. Shortly after 10.30 the manager announces a collective difference of $16,068.98. In three minutes more the receipt of correction tickets from fallible accountants reduces it to $70; in six minutes to $1.02, and in seven to $1. The discovery of that insidious dollar now engages the anxious energies of all the settling clerks and of the manager and his staff. In such a hunt no occult gifts of mind-reading are of any avail. The game eludes detection. "Exchange to the right for examination of footings!" is the next order, instantly followed by transfer of each settling sheet to the dexter neighbor, who runs up the arithmetical columns. But the cunning dollar is not unearthed. "Bank of New York and Ninth National lead off for examination. Both amounts with care!" is the following command from the chief. Another orderly evolution ensues, in which debits and credits are called off, but without the desired result. Fresh tactics are adopted, and the caller in turn plays the part of listener. Still no discovery. At 11.05, "Change sheets to the left!" is the curt instruction, and sheets are changed to the left. "Ah! there it is. An error in both columns." The fugitive is captured, penned up in correction ticket, conveyed in triumph to the proof clerk, deposited in the correction column, and proof is once more proclaimed.

No.	Banks.	Due Clearing House.	Banks. Dr.	Banks. Cr.	Due Banks.	No.
1	Bank of N. Y. Nat'l B'k'g Ass'n.	$678,681.89	$10,235,874.46	$9,167,102.59	....	1
2	Manhattan Company............	....	7,494,330.05	7,535,548.16	$41,218.11	2
3	Merchants' National Bank.....	....	2,724,144.49	2,771,699.57	47,555.08	3
4	Mechanics' National Bank.....	....	2,093,405.14	2,102,470.73	9,065.59	4
5	Union National Bank...........	....	5,103,057.77	5,140,549.71	37,491.94	5
6	Bank of America...	130,281.90	3,422,414.62	3,392,131.81	....	6
7	Phœnix National...............	....	702,227.00	104,504.57	202,307.51	7
8	National City Bank............	226,506.06	3,857,227.89	3,680,741.83	....	8
83	Seaboard Bank.................	42,301.04	1,641,982.90	1,509,021.86	....	83
86	Sixth National Bank...........	....	55,321.40	71,731.43	16,410.03	86
87	Western National Bank........	....	....	....	....	87
	Numbers, names, and amounts from 8 to 85 omitted.	$4,301,201.77	$124,993,869.38	$124,993,869.38	$4,301,201.77	

SPECIMEN CLEARING HOUSE PROOF.

In an hour and a half—ordinarily in three-quarters of an hour—from the time of beginning, unbroken silence reigns in the deserted clearing room. What has been faultily done therein is soon ascertained at the fiscal institution, whose representative has subjected its treasury to an exaction of six dollars by the commission of a double error. Only forty-five minutes are allowed for effecting proof. Errors undetected at 11.15 are mulcted by a double fine, at 12 M. by one quadrupled. For all errors on the credit side of the settling-clerk's statement, whether of entry or footing, of the *amounts brought*, and for all discrepancies between credit-entries, check-tickets, and exchange-slips, a fine of $3 each is imposed; for every error in making entries of the amounts received, $2; for errors in the tickets reported to the clearing house, and causing differences between the balances and the aggregate, $2 each; errors in footing receipts, $1 (rarely inflicted); disorderly conduct or non-compliance with managerial mandates, each offence, $2; failure to be punctually on hand with statements and tickets complete, at the morning exchanges, $2; neglect of debtor banks to pay their balances before 1.30 P. M., $3; and for each mistake in the delivery or receipt of exchanges, $1. Part of the painfully interesting correspondence of the member banks is the manager's monthly report of its fines.

PARK NATIONAL BANK.

SETTLING CLERK'S STATEMENT. Nov. 1, 1888.

No.	Banks	First Debit.	Additions.	Total Debit.	Banks Cr.	No.
1	Bank of New York Nat'l. Banking Ass'n.	$1,220,589 89	$100,087 22	$1,320,877 17	$1,296,732 11	1
2	Manhattan Co......	556,781 00	....	556,781 00	693,829 25	2
Sixty-three other bank accounts omitted.						
	Footings.........	$6,337,229 10	$125,333 25	$6,462,562 35	$6,241,410 35	
			Credit Balance......	221,152 00		
				$6,241,410 35		

SPECIMEN SETTLING CLERKS' STATEMENT.

CHAPTER XVII.

BANK OF ENGLAND AND AMERICAN BANK NOTES.

Description of a Bank of England Note—How Made—Peculiarity of Design—Number of Notes Paid Out Daily and Number Cancelled—How Burned and Destroyed—The Accountant's Library—Why Notes are Not Reissued—The Bank's Printing Office—Durability of the Notes—Cutting Notes in Two Pieces Sent Through the Mails—Curiosities in the Bank Album—Barlow's Remarks on Bank of England Notes—Antiquity of Bank Notes—United States Currency—How it is Printed, Worn Out and Destroyed—Workings of the National Bank Redemption Agency.

NOTWITHSTANDING Bank of England notes are to be found in all parts of the world, there are undoubtedly many people who have never seen one, and following will be found a brief description:—

They are unlike any other note in the world. In size they are quite large, being about 8½ inches in length by 5½ in width, and of a design plain and unpretending in the highest degree. The ink used in printing is of an intense black, upon paper of remarkable whiteness, which is also extremely crisp and tough.

The Bank of England note is printed on Irish linen water-lined paper, plain white and with ragged edges. The paper lacks the smooth, oily feeling of United States currency, and the plainness of the lettering and the entire absence of any coloring excepting black and white makes the bill in appearance easy to counterfeit.

The chief object in the manufacture of bank notes is to render forgery impossible, or at least easy of detection. This is sought to be effected by peculiarity of paper, design, and printing, or by a combination of these means. The main reliance in the case of the notes of the Bank of England has been on mechanical design; the writing, the emblems, and the ornaments being so combined as to render forgery difficult. The ink, too, is peculiar, being the blackest and the most indelible of inks. As a further security against forgery, a self-registering machine is used. Copperplate printing was the only printing in use for bank notes till 1837, when a great improvement was made. This was the production of designs by the mill and die by mechanical pressure. The pattern is engraved on a soft steel plate, which is then hardened, to transfer the pattern by pressure to a soft steel roller, on which, of course, the pattern is produced in relief; the roller or mill is then hardened, to reproduce the pattern in the plate from which the printing is to be done; and thus almost any number of plates for all common purposes can easily be produced. No Bank of England notes are issued twice. This system of siderography continued in use for bank note printing in the Bank of England till 1855, when electrotype printing was introduced by Mr. Smee, with the assistance of the mechanical officials; and since that time the notes of the Bank of England have been all produced by surface-printing by the electrotype. The whole of the printing of the bank is executed within its walls. The number of persons employed in the printing department solely on the production of notes is about thirty. In addition to these there are nine cashiers and sub-cashiers, who are highly paid officers of the bank.

Of the paper required in the manufacture of bank notes about 15,000 reams are usually supplied to the bank yearly, each ream of 500 pieces of paper making 1,000 notes, the paper being generally kept for six months before it is taken into use. The paper is made at a special manufactory at a cost of about £1 a ream. The dies from which the water-mark is made, as well as the plates used in printing the notes, are all manufactured at the bank, where also the notes are printed. The chief cashier regulates the quantity of notes required to be printed, and sends orders to the printing office for the number he deems requisite. The notes, which were formerly printed by the distinct process, are now completed by one operation. They are placed in the hands of the cashiers, who count them over, and discharge the printer of all further responsibility.

The Bank of England never re-issues its notes. As they come in they are laid aside, and kept five years and then burned. The whole number is not destroyed together, but at different times, and as many are burnt as corresponds with the new notes issued. Notes are issued to anyone in exchange for gold or other notes. The notes are generally issued to bankers in bundles containing five hundred each. For every note issued an entry has previously been made recording its number and the date of issue. This entry is not closed until the note is returned to the bank and cancelled. The note may be out for years, or only for a few hours; in any case, the book in which it has been entered is kept open to receive the completion of its history. Ordinarily about 50,000 notes are paid by the bank in a day, and about as many new ones are issued. Those which have been in circulation are at once cancelled, the corner bearing the signature of the cashier being torn off, and the words indicating the denomination punched out. The number of notes thus cancelled daily varies from 30,000 to nearly 80,000, and averages about 50,000. When they are thus cancelled, and have been accounted for in the books, they are arranged according to their numbers and date in parcels of from 300 to 1,500, and are marked in such a way with references to the balance sheets that a clerk can readily ascertain by whom and when each was paid in. The parcels are then deposited in the accountant's library, and preserved for five years, at the end of which they are burned. The accountant's library usually contains nearly one hundred millions of these cancelled notes stowed away in about 13,500 boxes, any one of which can be referred to in four or five minutes.

While this system is very expensive it is not deemed extravagant, because of the great advantages it offers. The most notable advantage is the cleanly condition of the circulation; but of course there are other advantages of greater import. One is the facility with which the payment of any note is traced, and also the saving of labor in keeping account of the notes. In this all the London bankers share, as none of them pay out any but new notes. All notes received by them in the course of their business are paid in to their accounts at the Bank of England, and they draw new notes for their requirements. In paying away large bundles of notes they are able to keep a record of their distinctive numbers by entering only the numbers of the first and last of the parcel. The plan of re-issuing notes was tried by the bank in 1838, but so much inconvenience was caused to the bankers and the public that it was abandoned. It seems to be a very wasteful proceeding that a quantity of newly manufactured notes issued by the bank in the forenoon, and returned to the bank in the afternoon, should not be re-issued, but stored away and eventually consigned to the flames.

No notes of a higher denomination than £1000 are issued, and, as the bank's printing press is capable of producing these at the rate of 3000 an hour, this part of its work is soon accomplished. There are several other presses printing five and ten pound notes, some completing with one, and those of older date with two impressions. The number and date of each note are printed at both ends of it, and as the separate halves are thus easily identified, it is common in England to remit money by cutting a bank-note in two equal pieces and transmitting each by different mails or in separate envelopes. This is done as a guard against theft and loss. A portion of the bill has no value. Not the smallest scrap of paper is wasted, and if a note is spoiled in the printing, it has to be accounted for no less than the perfect ones.

While for beauty of design the notes of the Bank of England are inferior to those of the United States, they are securer and more durable. Brittle to the touch as the paper seems, it is almost as strong as parchment, and it is possible to hold a piece no larger than a note by the edges and place a fifty-pound weight upon it without tearing it. Its thinness and transparency prevent erasures and other illegal alterations.

In an album kept at the bank the various counterfeits discovered are preserved, and the best of these is one executed by a Frenchman. It would take an extremely experienced eye to detect any fault in the engraving, but the spuriousness of the paper is visible at a glance. Most of the imitations could not deceive a child, and the poorest one shown in the bank is a hundred pound note which was sent to a charitable institution inclosed with a benevolent letter.

The penalty for forgery is so heavy, and the detectives of the Bank of England are so vigilant, that few criminals have courage enough to exercise their ingenuity in forging notes, and at the present time no forged notes are known to be in circulation. In earlier times, when the design of the notes was ruder, forgery could be attempted with greater impunity, and the history of the bank, like all old and large financial institutions, contains many instances of daring and brilliant roguery.

The bank album, in which specimens of the various counterfeits discovered are preserved, also contains some interesting proofs of the extraordinary durability of the notes. There are three notes for twenty-five pounds which passed through the Chicago fire and were sent in for redemption. Though they are burnt to a crisp black ash, the paper is scarcely broken, and the engraving is as clear as in a new note. There are also five five-pound notes which went to the bottom of the sea in the unfortunate training ship, "Eurydice," and were recovered after six months' immersion. They are not even frayed. The paper is stained a light brown, and that is the only effect their long exposure to salt water has had. In a small case, covered with a magnifying glass, are a few charred fragments of paper, for which the bank paid £1,400. They are the remains of several notes destroyed in a fire, and were redeemed at their full value, the holders being able to give their numbers and dates, and to satisfy the bank that they had actually been destroyed. There is another note in the album, which was in circulation 125 years before it was returned to the bank for payment. As soon as a note is returned, even though it has been out but a few hours, it is cancelled. Very often a note issued in the morning is brought back to the bank in the afternoon of the same day; but on an average a five-pound note is out about eighty days. One thing the notes will not endure. They will hold together at the bottom of the sea, and come out of a furnace intact, but they will not outlast the scrubbing, the bleaching and the mangling of the laundry.

A Bank of England note is the safest piece of paper in the world, and, under any circumstances, the bank could pay every one in circulation without touching a shilling of its capital. The great object of the charter of 1844 was to secure at all times and under every possible contingency the conversion of every bank note into gold whenever presented for payment, and that object has been completely attained. The effect has been to accumulate much more gold than would have been necessary had the interests of the shareholders alone been considered; and while this stock of bullion, bearing no interest, and held only for the integrity of the bank note, is a drawback from one point of view, the enormous benefit which the country derives from the absolute equality of the note and the coin far outweighs any attendant disadvantage.

The following curious description of the paper used in making bank notes is abridged from Barlow's lecture on "A Bank of England Note."

"The color of the paper is peculiar, and cannot exactly be imitated by a forger, except at great expense. The combined thinness and strength of the paper is also unique. The paper is made in pieces large enough for two notes; each note before it is sized weighs about eighteen grains, and if then doubled it is strong enough to suspend a weight of thirty-six pounds; with the addition of about a grain of size it will suspend fifty-six pounds. The texture of the paper is also peculiar; it has a crisp feel, invariably the same, and such that bank clerks of experience can readily detect forgeries by this test alone."

Those who suppose that bank notes are a modern invention may be surprised to know that they were first issued in China more than two thousand years before Christ. They were engraved in blue ink on paper made from the fibres of the mulberry tree, and had on them this motto: "Produce all you can; spend with economy." Besides this were designs similar to those of modern notes, such as the date of issue, number of note, signature of the official issuing it, and also a notice of the pains and penalties of counterfeiting. One of these curiosities is preserved in the Asiatic Museum at St. Petersburg, and bears the date equivalent to 1399 B. C.

United States paper currency is more artistic in appearance and convenient in size and form than Bank of England notes.

The Bureau of Engraving and Printing, at Washington, D. C., where all United States currency is manufactured, occupies a large brick building built expressly for it, at a cost of some $300,000. It has three stories and a high basement. Here 250 plate presses are worked by hand, and over 500 men and women employed in the processes of printing sheets of bank notes, bonds and internal revenue stamps. Six hundred sheets per day are printed on each press, and after each impression the delicate copper and steel plate must be removed from the press, carefully wiped dry, polished with whiting, inked and then returned to its place for another impression. The fibre paper must be handled expertly, and everything about the work done with precision and care. All is perfect system and exactness here. The greenbacks and other securities issued for the government, from the time the paper is manufactured until the finished note is issued, are subjected to a system of registering and checking at every step, so minute and precise that the chance of any error or dishonesty in the handling of this most valuable product is reduced to a minimum.

The sheets before being wet are delivered to the plate printers, counted and charged to them, and again counted in the presence of an assistant, who certifies to the count. Attached to the machines by which the wetting is done are registers which automatically count the sheets a third time as they pass through. Next comes the examining division, where, after the fourth count, the sheets are dried and counted for the fifth time. Experts then examine the sheets, and those which are pronounced perfect go into the hydraulic press, from which powerful machine they emerge in a smooth state ready for printing.

Any sheets spoiled in printing—too light or too dark, or otherwise imperfect—are thrown out by the examiner, but cannot be destroyed until after passing through a regular prescribed course. The lettering and numbering divisions, and the engraving division, are interesting also. Visitors are permitted to inspect all the divisions of the bureau, and a guide is provided to conduct all who apply on a "tour" of the rooms. Of the 500 or 600 persons employed, a large majority are ladies, and some of the most difficult and responsible work is performed by lady experts. The bureau turns out an average of $100,000 in notes printed daily. The great chilled iron and steel vaults of the treasury are objects of much interest, but only certain ones can be entered by outsiders, and these only on a permit from the treasurer.

When the national bank notes have tramped about the country until they have become ragged and vagabond, and have reached the lowest depths of degradation, they are bundled up and sent to the Treasury Department for redemption. Many millions of these vagrants are received at the department each year. They have to pass in review through the National Bank Redemption Agency, where those that are utterly depraved and good for nothing are sentenced to be chewed up, and those which have got in through the force of association, but are still not so far gone that some good may not be got out of them, are sent back into the service. In the place of those that are condemned nice, new notes, crisp and clean, are sent out. The experience of these notes is varied, and in some cases very novel and interesting, but their tale is told only by their ragged and dirty appearance when they get back to the department. The average length of time that a new note can keep up a respectable appearance is about three years. Some have been found at the end of twenty years to be as crisp as on the day of their issue, but these are exceptional cases, where they have fallen into the hands of people who made pets of them, and carefully guarded them from rough usage. The wandering note soon becomes a tramp. It rapidly goes to pieces if it starts out for the west, stopping along at the crossroad inns, or if it frequents drinking saloons and falls in with low company. Bad habits tell on a bank note very quickly. It is in hard luck when it falls in with a bloody-fingered butcher. Some have been known to become good for nothing under such circumstances in a few weeks. They are subject, too, to all sorts of misfortune by fire and water.

Many thousand get burned up. Then their charred and blackened remains are sent to the treasury for redemption. One lady in the comptroller's office in this case has charge of them, and they are sent to her for identification before they can be redeemed. She is said to be very expert, seldom failing to identify a note, giving its proper name, date and classification, no matter how badly burned it is. Sometimes packages of several hundred, done up to be expressed, are sent in all stuck together, and burned clear through to a black crispy mass. She then separates them one by one with a very thin bladed knife, and places the charred remains of each one separately on a glass slab and examines it very carefully with a magnifying glass. She is familiar with all peculiarities of the issues of the various banks, and the note must be reduced almost to ashes to be beyond her recognition, though to an experienced eye it might not be distinguished from a piece of grocer's paper which had gone through the fire.

All these notes otherwise mutilated go directly to the Redemption Agency. The degree of expert efficiency displayed there is something remarkable. This branch of the service was organized by General Spinner. Prior to that there was no systematic redemption of the paper currency as it became too worn for circulation, and a good many ragamuffin notes were wandering about the country.

The counting-in and assorting of the notes requires great care, and it is only after long experience that it can be done rapidly. There is an average of about 150,000,000 notes per year handled, and they have to be counted about five hundred times, if there is no hitch in the count, and oftener if any mistakes are made.

The force can handle just half a million notes each day. This is very expert counting. The notes, when they come to be judged, have first to be "counted-in." This requires the "counters-in" to go over them twice, and they must make no mistake and pass no counterfeit, or the loss thus caused will be deducted from their salaries. To do this requires constant attention and is a great strain on the nerves, as each note has to be scrutinized very closely to see that it is not counterfeit, and the "counter-in" must know the name of every bank that has a counterfeit upon it, and have in his mind a full description of the false note, so as to be able to detect it at sight. The superintendent says counterfeit notes are thrown out by these experts without hesitation every time they come to them. They have a line of notes passing before their eyes at the time, and any flaw or defect they notice on the instant. So familiar is everyone with the money of the United States that an extended description would not be particularly interesting or instructive.

CHAPTER XVIII.

ISSUE DEPARTMENT,—NO INTEREST ON DEPOSITS.

Preparing Bank Notes for Use—How Notes Get into Circulation—Exchanging Notes for Gold—Inland and Foreign Withdrawals—The Bullion Office—Bank of England Purchasing Gold—Gold Weighing Room—Mechanical Accuracy and Dispatch—No Interest Allowed on Deposits—An Ex-Governor Defends the Policy of the Bank—A Tradition.

As PREVIOUSLY stated, the paper upon which Bank of England notes are printed is specially made for the bank, and the greatest care is taken to produce a paper that is difficult to counterfeit. As fast as the paper is printed it is sent to the bank and placed under the care of the chief cashier. The notes are then printed at the bank and kept in the banking department until wanted in the Issue Department. Each note bears the date of its printing, together with a distinctive number.

One of the great divisions of the functions of the Bank of England is the Issue Department. This operation is carried on under the immediate supervision of the chief cashier, who is responsible that the conditions imposed upon the bank by the Act of 1844 are strictly complied with. The first requisite of a practical nature is the preparation of the notes themselves, which is fully described in Chapter XVII.

When the chief cashier from time to time orders the issue of fresh bank notes, he gives the chief accountant notice thereof, specifying how many are to be prepared, and the dates they will respectively bear. The accountant immediately opens a general credit for the amount of the new creation of notes, and at the same time prepares books in his own department, called ledgers, numbered and dated to correspond with the notes in question, in which a separate credit is opened for every individual note made.

The notes being now ready for use are drawn from the treasury, as occasion may require, by the chief cashier, whether for London or branch bank issues, and passed into the Issue Department, from which they are issued to the public, to the bankers, to the banking offices of the house, and to the respective branches, so that this department is cognizant of, and virtually responsible for, the issue of all the notes circulated by the Bank of England. There are two principal ways in which notes get into circulation. In the first place, notes are issued to anyone in exchange for gold bullion; and, secondly, any person having a drawing account at the bank has only to draw a cheque, and on its presentation he will be paid the whole or any part of the amount on his account in notes, or notes and gold, as he may prefer. Every note issued is entered by its number and date in the books of the Issue Department, and these books being all duly balanced at the close of each day, all the remaining notes (including those considered as broken cash, in the hands of the pay-clerks, and deposited each night in the treasury) are returned every evening to the cashier, whose account will then show the number of notes issued in the course of the day. Simultaneously with this process, another will have been in operation through the day, and in the same department, viz., the exchange of notes for gold. The bank note being a promise to pay the amount thereof in gold on demand, anyone bringing notes to the bank is entitled to make his demand, and during each day large amounts of gold are given in exchange for notes. The cashier's daily account, therefore, will show the number of notes received back again by the bank in this way, as well as all paid in to account by parties having drawing accounts at the bank. A similar account in abstract of all notes exchanged for gold, or gold exchanged for notes, and of notes paid or received in the banking offices, is kept by the accountant of the bank, whose accounts must agree daily with those of the cashier.

It is evident that the amount of bank notes issued varies in exact proportion to the amount of gold in the Issue Department, the issue against the government debt and other securities being invariable. Roughly speaking, the contraction or expansion of the circulation indicates a corresponding curtailment or increase in commercial facilities or requirements. Hence the Issue Department return becomes an important guide to the operations of bankers, brokers, and financial firms, by whom it is carefully watched, since the increase or diminution of the stock of gold may be said respectively to be a signal of safety or danger. The receipts or withdrawals of gold in any large quantity by and from the bank are of two kinds, inland and foreign. The former for the most part occurs at certain regular periods of the year, such as the harvest season, Scotch "term-time," etc. They exercise but a very modified and temporary influence on the money market, for the laws by which they are governed are fairly understood and recognized, and the amount of gold actually in the kingdom remains unaltered.

It has already been mentioned that as the notes are from time to time numbered and dated for issue, the accountant is made acquainted therewith, and that he prepares ledgers containing a separate credit for every note issued. When the notes are returned again to the bank for payment, these individual credits are cancelled by the date of the return of each respective note being posted in the ledger against the number corresponding with that borne by the note itself. Thus it will be seen that the amount of the credits closed, or, in other words, the number of notes paid in, being deducted from the circulation account, will show at the close of each day the actual number and amount of the notes remaining in circulation.

Another important part of the bank, directly connected with the Issue Department, is the bullion office. As the Bank of England is bound by law to buy any amount of gold at the rate of £3 17s. 9d. per ounce of standard gold, or, in other words, to give its notes or acknowledgement at that rate, it is necessary to have a department where the bullion so acquired may be placed in safe custody. The obligation on the bank to buy gold or bullion at the above mentioned rate per ounce standard is a convenience to the public who require an exchangeable commodity such as coin, instead of gold as imported, in the shape of bullion—bullion meaning gold or silver in any other shape or form than coin. If an importer of gold wishes to sell, that is, to obtain gold coin which he can pay away, he can take his bullion to the mint, and for every ounce of gold of twenty-two carats fine, or twenty-two parts out of twenty-four pure gold, he will receive gold coin at the rate of £3 17s. 10½d. per ounce; but to obtain this he must send the gold to the mint, and wait some weeks for the coin. It is, therefore, found more advantageous to the seller to take the gold to the bank and receive 1½d. less per ounce; this operation being effected without any loss to the bank, which sells again the same bullion at the rate of £3 17s. 10½d. per ounce, or obtains sovereigns from the mint. The bank only sends its bullion to the mint as it may be in want of gold coin. Frequently it sells foreign gold coin at a small profit, as it may be worth more to an exporter—for instance, to Russia—to have Russian gold coin than either bar gold or sovereigns; but, in all cases, the general rule of the bank is to buy foreign gold coin only at such a price as will render it equivalent to gold bars—that is to say, at a rate for which, without loss, it can always convert such coin into bars at £3 17s. 9d. per ounce standard, which again can be converted into British gold coin at the mint.

The bullion office at the bank is also made use of as a depot or warehouse for gold or silver, or other such valuable commodities—diamonds or precious stones, for instance; and importers are allowed to deposit and retire their goods free of charge, the bank being remunerated by small payments for the use of the bank's scales and packing bullion for export.

All gold paid into the bank is weighed in a room called the "Gold Weighing Room." In this room there are sixteen machines (the invention of Mr. Cotton, a former governor of the bank) constantly at work. It is merely necessary to keep them fed with sovereigns and half-sovereigns, and the whole process of weighing and dividing the light from the full-weight coins is performed automatically by the machines, at the rate of about 2,000 an hour each, and with an accuracy and precision that could not possibly be attained by manual labor. In this manner, in the year 1885, £25,087,250 worth of gold coin was weighed and sorted, and the number of individual pieces amounted to 27,272,760. As each gold coin paid into the bank is very accurately weighed, to the daily average of about 89,125, and those found to be light are cut, the current weight of the circulation is to a considerable extent preserved.

The machines are kept in motion by an atmospheric engine, connected with the steam engine, and the light coins are immediately cut, to be remelted.

The Bank of England does not allow, either at the head office in London, or at its branches, any interest on deposits, and many plausible reasons have been advanced in defence of this rule. Mr. Wegeulin, formerly governor of the bank, gave the views of the managers of that institution on interest on deposits before a parliamentary committee in 1857.

He said the managers of the Bank of England have always considered that the "proper functions of a banker were to keep the spare cash of his customer, such cash as his customer required for his daily expenditure, for the sudden demands of his business, and any accidental accumulation which might happen before the customer had occasion to invest it. That is contrasted with the system pursued by the joint-stock banks. The joint-stock bank invites a large deposit by offering a certain rate of interest for the deposit; in point of fact, the joint-stock bank becomes the investor of the money instead of the customer. The customer of a joint-stock bank does not himself invest his own money, but he employs the joint-stock bank to do it, taking the guarantee of the joint-stock bank, and taking, possibly, a lower rate of interest. Now, that system, if applied to the Bank of England, would be very prejudicial to the public interests. It would, in the first place, force upon the Bank of England to invest its reserves much more closely than it does now. If it had to pay interest upon its deposits, it could only do so by investing them in some securities that would pay a higher rate of interest than that which it pays. Its deposits also are of that particular character which would render it still more inexpedient that they should be closely invested. They consist, in the first place, of government deposits, which rise from a low rate at one period of a quarter up to five or six millions higher at another period of a quarter, and again collapse to a very low rate at another period. Again, the private deposits consist, to a certain extent, of the deposits of the bankers and the joint-stock banks of London. Those deposits are the amounts which those bankers require to work their own business. Consequently, they are not deposits which should be very closely invested by the Bank of England."

A former officer of this bank says that, in times when there is a great accumulation of deposits in the Bank of England, it is because the public are not able at those times to find investments to their mind to employ those deposits; and consequently, it is not at all likely that the Bank of England, if that is the case with the public generally, will be able to find investments which the public themselves have not been able to do. All these reasons combined would lead one to think, that to force a system upon the Bank of England by which it should be obliged to employ its deposits very closely—much more closely than it does at present—would be not only prejudicial and unsafe as regards the Bank of England, but would be prejudicial to the public interest.

It is, however, obvious that this reasoning is quite inconlusive. The truth is, says another ex-governor, that the non-allowance of interest is a tradition, of no authority in itself, and operating injuriously in keeping up the delusion that the banking department of the Bank of England is an institution differing essentially in the character of its business from other banks.

Equivalent of British Money in American Money.														
Shillings.	Dollars.	Cents.	Mills.	Shillings.	Dollars.	Cents.	Mills.	Shillings.	Dollars.	Cents.	Mills.	Pounds.	Dollars.	Cents.	Pounds.	Dollars.	Cents.
1		24.2		7	1	69.4		13	3	.14.6		1	4	84	15	72	60
2		48.4		8	1	93.6		14	3	.38.8		2	9	68	20	96	80
3		72.6		9	2	.17 8		15	3	.63.0		3	14	52	25	121	00
4		96.8		10	2	.42.0		16	3	.87.2		4	19	36	30	145	20
5	1	.21.0		11	2	.66.2		18	4	.35.6		5	24	20	35	169	40
6	1	.45.2		12	2	.90.4		20	4	.84.0		10	48	40	50	242	00

CHAPTER XIX.

PRESENT MANAGEMENT AND DESCRIPTION OF THE BANK OF ENGLAND.

How the Bank is Officered and Managed—Qualification and Election of Officers—Salaries—Tenure of Office—Court of Directors—Bank Committees—Explanation of their Duties—Division of the Clerical Force—Working in Harmony—The Secretary and his Duties—Total Number of Employees in the Bank—The Enormous Salary List—Conveniences and Societies for Clerks—Library, Reading and Dining Room—Insurance and Guarantee Society—Medical Attendance—How Clerks are Appointed—Names of the Various Departments—Description of the Bank—Its Exterior and Interior—Number of Acres the Bank Occupies—Statue in Bank, with Inscription Thereon—How the Bank is Guarded—Officers who Reside in the Bank—Eminent Services Rendered by the Bank.

THE management of the bank is entirely in the hands of the proprietors of the bank stock, and absolutely without any sort of interference or control on the part of the government. The direction of its affairs is committed to a committee composed of the governor, the deputy governor, and twenty-four directors. Eight of these directors retire annually, by rotation, and are all invariably re-elected, unless they wish to retire. In that case the court of directors submits to the proprietors the name or names of any persons whom it may be thought desirable to have upon the committee. The qualification for a director is the holding of £2,000 stock, and as the position is very much coveted, the names submitted are usually members of the very first firms in London. The governor and the deputy governor are also elected by the proprietors, although they are first selected by the directors from among themselves, and their names submitted to the general court at the annual meeting. The qualification for the position of governor is the holding of £4,000 stock, whilst the deputy governor must hold £3,000. The qualification of a proprietor for voting is the holding of £500 of stock in his own right. The governor and the deputy governor are elected for one year only, but as they are invariably re-elected at the close of the first year, they hold office for two years. At the expiration of that time, the governor returns upon the board of directors, and the deputy governor invariably succeeds and is elected governor, and a new deputy is chosen. The governor and deputy governor each receive £1,000 per annum, and every director receives £500 per annum. From the careful manner in which the directors are selected, it follows that the management of the bank, which really involves the most important interests of the whole commercial community, is conducted by men who are in touch with every movement of commerce and finance in the country, and in every quarter of the world.

Matters of daily routine, such as questions relating

to discipline, are generally referred, in the first instance, to the deputy governor; while all communications between the government and the bank, and all matters affecting the principle of management, are referred, usually, direct to the governor, who is the final appeal in all cases requiring decision, which the heads of departments may not consider themselves justified in settling.

The directors are in like manner elected annually by the proprietors; but although the stockholders in this way have the power of turning out any director—that is, of not re-electing him—yet, on vacancies occurring, it has been the invariable rule to leave the selection of new directors to the court of directors, which include all of the directors of the bank, and the governor and deputy governor, who are considered more competent to choose efficient members for the board, and who, from their position in business and general character, are best calculated to promote the important interests and general welfare of the Bank of England.

Beyond the status which their position gives them, the governor and deputy governor derive no benefit from their office, while they tax themselves most liberally by their contributions towards the welfare of their clerks. They remain in office for two years only, and this short tenure of office is, with considerable reason, thought to be detrimental to the efficient and consistent administration of the functions of government. A governor, let us say, is an enlightened financier; for two years his policy is paramount; but his successor then comes, and, perhaps, reverses everything, and the onus of the change, so far as the bank customers are concerned, is left to be borne by the permanent officers of the bank, who have, perhaps, never been consulted in the matter, or whose opinions, based on the experience of many years, may be ruthlessly ignored. The two years' system undoubtedly has its advantages in the constant introduction of new blood ; it also strengthens the governors from above and below the chair. The directors below the chair give the governor a loyal and hearty support, because they feel that one day their own turn may come, while those above the chair, having passed through the ordeal, know the value of their colleagues' support.

The governor and deputy governor are in daily attendance at the bank ; and there is also a daily committee, consisting of three directors, who meet at half-past eleven o'clock, to receive reports of all proceedings at the branches, see that the whole of the securities of the previous day have been lodged with the proper officers, take in or deliver gold or silver from the vaults, approve or reject bills offered for discount, examine from time to time securities deposited by customers, and attend generally to any work required by the governors.

The twenty-four directors in addition to the two governors, and these, collectively, constitute the court of directors. The court meets for regular business every Thursday, when a statement is made, showing the exact position of the bank accounts up to the preceding night, and when every matter is brought before it requiring its authority, such as the granting of discount accounts, the ordering of payments for lost notes, the granting of pensions, and all other matters which the governor has not authority to carry out on his own responsibility, as well as those which the governor thinks of sufficient importance to require communication to the directors.

The directors have full cognizance, either by direct weekly communication or otherwise, of every transaction carried on in the bank. The court of directors is divided into certain committees, whose duty it is to attend to all matters referred especially to their consideration, and who are required to report their proceedings from time to time to the court.

The regular committees are six in number:—

The committee of treasury.

The committee of daily waiting.

The committee for law suits and the management of the branch banks.

The committee for the house and servants and the examination of clerks.

The committee of inspection for the cashier's office.

The committee of inspection for the accountant's office.

In addition to which, special committees are from time to time appointed, as occasion may require.

The treasury committee consists of the two governors for the time being, the directors who have already filled those positions, and those who, without having served as governor, have been specially elected by the court to this committee.

The committee of daily waiting consists of three directors in rotation from the whole body. Their attendance is at half-past eleven o'clock daily, and they are required to remain until all that part of the business of the day which is usually referred to them is concluded. All bills offered for discount in London are submitted to this committee, and all bills discounted at the country branches, except local bills, are shown to them on the following day. They have likewise charge of all bullion not required by the cashiers for daily wants.

The committee for law suits and the management of the branch banks attend to all business arising from prosecutions relating to forgeries, etc., and to everything appertaining to the ordinary administration of the branches.

The committee for the house and servants and the examination of clerks examine and pass the tradesmen's bills and accounts, order the payment of the salaries of the clerks and of the pensions, and in addition, examine all candidates for admission into the service, and consider the periodical reports upon the recently elected clerks during their term of probation.

The clerical machinery of this vast hive is divided into the "cash side" and the "accountant's side." The former, under the immediate supervision of the chief cashier, comprises the transaction of all business where actual cash is concerned, together with the necessary bookkeeping which it involves ; the latter, under charge of the chief accountant, takes cognizance of all matters of pure bookkeeping, where no actual cash is concerned, such as those which relate to the national debt accounts, the registration of bank notes and kindred work. In olden times, these important divisions were kept much more distinct than they are at present. There was, years ago, a certain antagonism between the two chiefs, which, however, has long since disappeared, and they now live and work together in a state of remarkable harmony, without even fighting over the question of precedence, which the chief accountant is supposed to claim, mainly, it is said, on alphabetical grounds, because A comes before C. The supervision of each office on both "sides" of the bank is intrusted to a principal and assistant principal, who are accountable to the chief cashier or accountant, as the case may be, and afterwards to a commitee of directors.

The secretary is a separate officer of the bank. He nurses the charter, and sees that its forms and ceremonies are complied with. He also records the proceedings of the courts, summons and attends all committee meetings. The secretary waits upon the governors of the bank, performs all necessary literary work, puts the candidates for clerkship through their preliminary examination, collects income tax, grants orders to visit the bank, etc. His duties are multifarious and exacting.

In the secretary's office the loss of bank notes, bills, dividend warrants, etc., is registered, and all matters and correspondence arising out of them, is conducted. It may be mentioned that as many as 2,700 notes have been recorded as lost in the course of a single year. Applications for payment of lost notes, under indemnity, are also investigated, and the necessary declarations and bonds prepared.

Record is kept in the secretary's office of all the officers, clerks and others in the employ of the bank, with their salaries, securities, etc.; and it is the secretary's duty to prepare and issue to the various offices lists of the salaries and pensions for payment monthly or quarterly, as they become due.

The secretary conducts the examination of all candidates for admission into the service, and has under his control about one hundred newly-elected clerks, who are not at first attached to any particular office, but are lent to the different departments as their services are required.

The secretary has the control of the clerk of works' department, and records and generally supervises all contracts and expenditures connected therewith. He also examines and records all other expenses of the house, bringing the whole before the committee at their periodical meetings of inspection.

The business connected with the bank provident society, which was established many years ago, to promote life insurance among the members of the staff, and the payment of the annuitants on the directors' fund for widows of bank clerks and porters, are also included in the work of the office.

The extreme accuracy and dispatch with which the clerical labor involved in the business of the Bank of England is performed is almost marvelous, and reflects the highest credit on the administrative machinery of the bank. Every possible expedient is resorted to for the purpose of facilitating the work and guarding against errors.

The total number of employees in the Bank of England is upwards of 1,160 persons, including those at the head office and the branches, and counting in the clerks, porters, mechanics and those engaged in printing the notes. The annual salaries amount to about £300,000, or $1,500,000, besides pensions to superannuated officers which amount to about £45,000 more. The salaries to the governors and the directors amount to £14,000 per annum. Everything in and about the bank is conducted on a very liberal basis, and the aggregate of the annual expenses are something enormous. Officials, clerks and the general employees of the bank are generally well paid.

There is a well appointed library and reading room in the bank, and they are thoroughly supplied with the standard books, periodicals and papers of the world. The works of reference this library contains is second to none. There are about 18,000 volumes in the library. The directors are liberal in their contribution of money for these. It might also be well to state in its connection that there are also a Clerks' Widow's Fund, a fund established by the clerks with the assistance of the bank. We take the following from "Gilbart's Practical Treatise on Banking:"— "In the year 1841, the Bank of England took measures for discontinuing the system of requiring securities from the clerks. Every clerk subscribed annually two shillings per cent. upon the amount of his surety bond. When he had subscribed in the course of five years (or immediately if he chose) ten shillings per cent., the liability of his sureties ceased. Every new clerk subscribes, when admitted, ten shillings per cent. on the amount of the bond he would otherwise give. These contributions are invested in standard securities. This fund is fixed at £6,000. When at this amount, the interest is given to the clerks' widow's fund. When the claims have reduced the fund below £6,000, the interest goes to this fund until it has increased to this amount. If the claims reduce the fund so low as £4,700, then the clerks are required to make a further contribution until the fund is again raised to £6,000.

But this contribution is never more than two shillings per cent. per annum on the amount of their respective bonds."

Connected with the above is "The United Guarantee and Life Insurance Company," the object of which is to grant policies for fidelity of trust, combined with policies of insurance on life, or with deferred annuities or endowments. The bank also has an apartment where its employees can dine cheaply and well. The directors of the Bank of England at all times manifest a kindness and good will towards their clerks.

The Bank of England has a physician who attends daily and is called the medical officer. He looks after the health of the clerks and other employees. Every clerk, when appointed, is carefully examined, to ascertain the condition of his health. If he applies for leave of absence on the ground of ill health, he undergoes a medical examination. If absent from illness he is visited by the medical officer, who reports his condition to the bank officials. If a clerk complains that his employment is injurious to his health, he is examined, and in some cases his employment is changed. If a clerk applies for a pension on account of age or illness, he is also examined.

The clerical force of the Bank of England is employed on a strictly civil service or competitive plan. Young men employed in subordidate positions have time and again reached the limit, spending their entire lives in the service of the bank. Politics or favoritism cut no figure, and merit alone insures permanency and advancement.

Besides the governor, deputy governor and twenty-four directors, the Bank of England is officered by the following named departments, many of which are subdivided, until the business of the bank works as accurately and harmoniously as a well regulated clock :

Chief accountant, deputy accountant, assistant accountant ; chief cashier and deputy and assistant; secretary and deputy and assistant; discount office, branch banks office, bank note office, bank stock office, consols office, India office, register office, power of attorney office, unclaimed dividend office, cheque office, superintendent of cashiers' store, numbering and dating office, bullion office, bill office, public drawing office, private drawing office, securities office, solicitors, medical officer, architect, etc.

The Bank of England is one of the most revered of institutions, and the visitor to London regards it with little less awe than he feels when he looks on the halls in which the liberty of England was nursed at Westminster. Locally speaking, it is a centre of London; in a larger sense, it is the pivot of the world.

Lombard street, Cornhill, Cheapside, King William street and Queen Victoria street have their confluence here, and empty into an irregular space, with the Corinthian portico of the Royal Exchange on one side, the similar architecture of the Mansion House nearly opposite, and the front of the great monetary institution on the third. The jam of traffic in the streets about the bank at times becomes hopelessly entangled. The illustration of the bank given in this volume is first-class in every particular.

The Royal Exchange and the Mansion House have architectural pretensions, while the Bank of England has none whatever. The bank has no windows in either of its fronts, but receives light from above or from its courts. Its exterior gives one the impression of a strongly-built granite inclosure, treated with heavy Ionic decoration, pierced with a ponderous gate, and surrounded by a weighty iron railing, which separates it by a foot or two from the sidewalk. Like everything else in London, it is blackened by the soot-laden atmosphere, and its general aspect is unprepossessing. Within is a court yard, guarded by a sentinel or porter, arrayed in flowing crimson and gold lace, and bearing a staff. From this court yard there are doors or gates by which the various divisions of the inclosure are reached, all of them low, solidly constructed, and modest, and grouped about, in all, nine court yards. Of these, one contains one or two stalwart elms, which in early summer seem to fill the entire space of it with bright and luxuriant verdure, while beneath them is a fountain, a neat bit of soft, well-kept turf, and clusters and hedges of rhododendrons. The visitor is hardly prepared to find a green court yard, great robust trees, and the sentimental music of a fountain in the heart of the greatest bank in the world. Probably no other trees in the world grow in such expensive soil, and to the visitor who sees them for the first time the incongruity of their position is very striking.

The interior of the bank has little of special interest, and a description of same would be of no particular value to anyone. It is full of respectability and business. Its air is one of conservative solemnity and decorous activity, and the demeanor of its employees and various officials is saturated with formal propriety. The various halls are spacious and modern in appearance, and the transactions during business hours seldom involve any crowding. There are files of clerks paying out money and receiving money from all sorts of people, other clerks bending over ledgers with intense application, and bank messengers in waiting, who are dressed in swallow-tail coats of a delicate salmon-color, with silver buttons, flaming scarlet waistcoats, black trousers and high silk hats. So much is open to the world; and even if the spectator is provided with a director's order to view the bank—a privilege not loosely granted—there is little of real interest for him to see; everything is commonplace, stern and secure.

The citizen who passes it on his way to his business, the merchant who considers it as an edifice where he gets his bills discounted or lodges his cash for security, the banker who visits it daily, look on the immense building with an indifferent eye. Even to a stranger, its external appearance is almost lost in contemplating the nobler structures that surround it. The Bank of England occupies a few feet more than eight acres. When the visitor passes from building to building, and notes each place devoted to its separate uses, yet all of them links in one chain, he cannot fail to be affected with the grandeur of that body which can command so extensive a service. The first stone of the original building was laid in 1732, and later additions bring it to its present size. The bank measures on the south side 365 feet; on the west side, 440 feet; on the north side, 410 feet; and the east side, 245 feet. The principal entrance to the bank is from Threadneedle street, opening by a large arched gateway into a quadrangular paved court, with which all the leading communications are connected.

On the establishment of the bank in 1694, the directors engaged the hall of the Grocers' Company for the purposes of their business, and continued to occupy it until the year 1732, when, having made a proposition to the Grocers' Company for a renewal of their lease, the terms of which were not approved of, the directors were authorized to "build a new bank in Threadneedle street, and to erect an equestrian statue of King William before it."

In August, 1732, the foundation stone was laid, on which was the following inscription:—

"*The foundation of this building of the Bank of England was laid August 1st, 1732, in the sixth year of the reign of King George the Second. Sir Edward Bellamy, Knight and Alderman, Governor; the Honorable Horatio Townshend, Esq., Deputy Governor;*" together with the names of the several directors.

Soon after the completion of the building, the proprietors of the bank caused a statue to be erected in the great hall, in commemoration of its founder, with a latin inscription of which the following is a translation:—

> FOR RESTORING EFFICACY TO THE LAWS;
> AUTHORITY TO THE COURTS OF JUSTICE;
> DIGNITY TO PARLIAMENT;
> TO ALL HIS SUBJECTS THEIR RELIGION AND LIBERTIES;
> AND CONFIRMING THESE TO POSTERITY,
> BY THE SUCCESSION OF THE ILLUSTRIOUS HOUSE OF HANOVER
> TO THE BRITISH THRONE:
> TO THE BEST OF PRINCES, WILLIAM THE THIRD,
> FOUNDER OF THE BANK,
> THIS CORPORATION, FROM A SENSE OF GRATITUDE,
> HAS ERECTED THIS STATUE;
> AND DEDICATED IT TO HIS MEMORY
> IN THE YEAR OF OUR LORD 1734,
> AND THE FIRST YEAR OF THIS BUILDING.

In the basement of the bank are the barracks, wherein thirty-six soldiers are quartered from seven o'clock every evening until the next morning, for the protection of the bank. It has been the custom to quarter soldiers in the bank since the Lord George Gordon riots, when it was threatened by a mob. Besides these, is a body of watchmen, all whom are trained to the use of the ample arrangements provided for in case of fire.

The building occupied by the Bank of England bears an estimated rental of £70,000 a year. The two principal officers of the bank, the Chief Accountant and the Chief Cashier, have residences within its walls; and although it is understood that they or their deputies shall always be in their residence, the bank premises are never left without the superintendence of other responsible agents—clerks of character and standing being appointed to attend every night during the year, and on Sundays and on bank holidays.

The gradual enfranchisement of banking by the various enactments between 1826 and 1858, and the enormous progress which banking has since made throughout Great Britain, have, however, considerably lessened the value of the exclusive banking privileges accorded to the Bank of England, and, from a mere proprietor's point of view, it is quite possible that the Bank of England might profitably forego their charter altogether now that they are in no fear of losing it, and, so far as pure banking is concerned, they no longer enjoy a monopoly.

The eminent services of the Bank of England to the political, commercial and financial world, the integrity and success with which it has been conducted, has long ago been recognized by the whole world. Generations and centuries come and go, but the Bank of England remains and moves along with a stability and precision that is truly wonderful. The workings and history of the Bank of England one hundred years hence will be substantially the same as to-day.

CHAPTER XX.

ENGLISH AND SCOTCH BANKS.

Scotch Banks Not Affected by the Bank of England—First Scotch Bank—Its Founder—Capital and Distribution of Shares—Origin of British Linen Bank—Passing Through Commercial Crises—Minimum Deposit Received—Allowing Interest on Deposits—Responsibility of Shareholders—Superior Banking System—Taking Advantage of an Old Law—A Scotch Cash Credit—General Solidity of Scotch Banks—Responsibility of Bank Partners—Law on Attaching a Debtor's Property—Scotch and Irish Banks in London.

THE monopoly given to the Bank of England by parliament by the Act of 1708, preventing more than six individuals from entering into a partnership for carrying on the business of banking, did not extend to Scotland. In consequence of the exemption, many banking companies, with numerous bodies of partners, have existed for a lengthened period in that part of the empire.

The earliest banking institution in North Britain was the Bank of Scotland. It was projected by a Mr. John Holland, of London, assisted by William Paterson, founder of the Bank of England, and was established by Act of the Scotch Parliament, in 1694. It was known by the name of the Governor and Company of the Bank of Scotland, and modeled in many particulars after the Bank of England. Its original capital was £1,000,000, or £100,000 sterling, distributed in shares of £1,000 Scotch, or £63., 6s., 8d., sterling, each. In 1727 came the Royal Bank of Scotland; in 1746, the British Linen Company, for the purpose, as its name implies, of undertaking the manufacture of linen. But the views in which it originated were speedily abandoned, and it became a banking company only. In 1810 came the Commercial Bank, and in 1825 the National Bank. Joint-stock banks have been established freely. These Scotch banks have passed readily through commercial crises which have destroyed large numbers of such institutions in England. The affairs of the banks are uniformly conducted by a board of directors, annually chosen by shareholders. The Bank of Scotland began to issue £1 notes so early as 1704, and their issue has since been continued without interruption. In England no notes below £5 are issued.

All the Scotch banks receive deposits of as low a value as £10, and often lower, and allow interest upon them. The interest allowed by the banks upon deposits varies, from time to time, according to the variations in the currency rate of interest.

The Bank of Scotland and the Bank of England are almost identical in management and principle.

The bill creating the Bank of Scotland exempted its capital from all public burdens, and gave it the exclusive banking in Scotland for twenty-one years, or until 1716.

The objects for which the bank was instituted, and its mode of management, were intended to be, and have been in most respects, similar to those of the Bank of England. The responsibility of the shareholders is limited to the amount of their shares. The capital of the bank was increased to £200,000 in 1774, and in 1804 was made £1,500,000, its present amount, although the capital was increased to £3,000,000 in 1873, by private act.

The Bank of Scotland is the only Scotch bank constituted by Act of Parliament. It began at a very early period to receive deposits on interest, and to grant credit on cash accounts, a minute of the directors with respect to the mode of keeping the latter being dated as far back as 1729. It is, therefore, entitled to the credit of having introduced and set on foot the distinctive principles of the Scotch banking system, which, whatever may be its defects, is superior to most other systems hitherto established. Generally speaking, the Bank of Scotland has been cautiously and skilfully conducted; and there can be no doubt that it has been productive, both directly and as an example to other banking establishments, of much public utility and advantage.

It may be worth mentioning that the law creating the Bank of Scotland declared that all foreigners who became partners in the bank, should by doing so become, to all intents and purposes, naturalized Scotchmen. After being for a long time forgotten, this clause was taken advantage of in 1818, when several aliens acquired property in the bank in order to secure the benefit of naturalization. But after being suspended, the privilege was finally cancelled in 1822.

The loans or advances made by the Scotch banks are either in the shape of discounts, or upon cash credits, or, as they are more commonly termed, "cash accounts."

A cash credit is a credit given to an individual by a banking company for a limited sum, seldom under £100 or £200, upon his own security, and that of two or three individuals approved by the bank, who become securities for its payment. The individual who has obtained such a credit is enabled to draw the whole sum, or any part of it, when he pleases, replacing it, or portions of it, according as he finds it convenient, interest being charged upon such part only as he draws out.

Joseph Hume, in his *Essay on Balance of Trade,* says: "If a man borrows £5,000 from a private hand, besides that it is not always to be found when required, he pays interest for it whether he be using it or not. His bank credit costs him nothing, except during the moment it is of service to him, and this circumstance is of equal advantage, as if he had borrowed money at a much lower rate of interest."

This is plainly one of the most commodious forms in which advances can be made. Cash credits are not, however, intended to be "dead loans;" and they are not granted except to persons in business, or to those who are frequently drawing out and paying in money.

The system of cash credits has been very well described in the report of the Lords' Committee of 1826, on Scotch and Irish banking. "There is, also," say their lordships, "one part of their system which is stated by all the witnesses to have had the best effects upon the people of Scotland, and particularly upon the middling and poorer classes of society, in producing and encouraging habits of frugality and industry. The practice referred to is that of cash credits. Any person who applies to a bank for a cash credit is called upon to produce two or more competent sureties, who are jointly bound; and after a full inquiry into the character of the applicant, the nature of his business, and the sufficiency of his securities, he is allowed to open a credit, and to draw upon the bank for the whole of its amount, or for such part as his daily transactions may require. To the credit of the account he pays in such sums as he may not have occasion to use, and interest is charged or credited upon the daily balance, as the case may be. From the facility which these cash credits give to all the small transactions of the country, and from the opportunities which they afford to persons who begin business with little or no capital but their character, to employ profitably the minutest products of their industry, it cannot be doubted that the most important advantages are derived to the whole community. The advantage to the banks that give these cash credits arises from the call which they continually produce for the issue of their paper, and from the opportunity which they afford for the profitable employment of a part of their deposits."

The expense of a bond for a cash credit of £500 is 12s. 6d. stamp duty, and a charge of from 5s. to 10s. 6d. per cent. for preparing it.

There have been, on the whole, comparatively few failures among the Scotch banks. In 1793 and 1825, when so many of the English banks were swept off, there was not a single establishment in Scotland that gave way. It is thought, however, that the long familiarity of the inhabitants with banks and paper money, and the less risk that has attended the business of banking in Scotland, have been the principal causes of the greater stability of the Scotch banks.

This superior solidity appears to have been owing to various causes,— partly to the banks having, for the most part, large bodies of partners, who, being conjointly and individually bound for the debts of the companies to which they belong, go far to render their ultimate security all but unquestionable, and partly to the facility afforded by the law of Scotland of attaching a debtor's property, whether it consist of land or movables, and making it available for the payment of his debts.

A creditor in Scotland is empowered to attach the real and heritable as well as the personal estate of his debtor, for payment of personal debts, among which may be classed debts due by bills and promissory notes ; and recourse may be had, for the purpose of procuring payment, to each description of property at the same time. Execution is not confined to the real property of a debtor merely during his life, but proceeds with equal effect upon that property after his decease.

The law relating to the establishment of records gives ready means of procuring information with respect to the real and heritable estate of which any person in Scotland may be possessed. No purchase of an estate in that country is secure until the sasine (that is, the instrument certifying that actual delivery has been given) is put on record, nor is any mortgage effectual until the deed is in like manner recorded.

In the case of conflicting pecuniary claims upon real property, the preference is not regulated by the date of the transaction, but *by the date of its record.* These records are accessible to all persons; and thus the public can with ease ascertain the effective means which a banking company possesses of discharging its obligations; and the partners in that company are enabled to determine, with tolerable accuracy, the degree of risk and responsibility to which the private property of each is exposed.

English joint-stock banks of issue are debarred from setting up branches in London, or within sixty-five miles of it, a prohibition originally imposed on them in the interest of the Bank of England as a bank of issue. There is no such prohibition affecting Scotch and Irish banks, which can set up offices in London or elsewhere in England subject to the single condition affecting all banking establishments set up in England since 1844, that notes other than Bank of England notes are not issued at such offices; and it is obvious that a Scotch or Irish banking company establishing a head office in London would be able to give it at once a large agency business, and would be able to feed it continuously with new connections, owing to the flow of immigration from Scotland and Ireland to London. Accordingly, the directors of the National Bank of Ireland began to conduct the general business of banking at their head office in London in 1854, and they have subsequently set up branches in the metropolis, each of which is understood to be the centre of much business. This example was so far followed, that the National Bank of Scotland started an office in London in 1864; the Bank of Scotland did the same in 1867; and the Royal Bank in 1874, and others followed later.

CHAPTER XXI.

A FINANCIAL PRESSURE.

Definition of a Pressure—Dates of Principal Pressures—Speculation the Main Cause—Gilbart on Pressures—The Duties of a Banker—Pressure of 1847—Report of the Lords' Committee—The Government Asks the Bank of England for Assistance—Correspondence Between the Bank and the Government.

A PRESSURE on the money market may be defined a difficulty of getting money, either by way of discounting bills, or of loans upon government securities. This difficulty is usually accompanied by an unfavorable course of exchange, a contraction of the circulation of the Bank of England, and a high rate of interest. These three circumstances have the relation to each other of cause and effect. The unfavorable course of exchange induces the Bank of England to contract her circulation; and the contraction of the circulation, by rendering money more scarce, increases its value, and leads to an advanced rate of interest. The removal of the pressure is in the same order—the foreign exchange become favorable, the Bank of England then extends her circulation, money becomes more abundant, and the rate of interest falls. The degree to which the exchanges are unfavorable is indicated by the stock of gold in the Bank of England; and when this is at its lowest amount, the pressure may be considered to have attained its extreme point; for, as the amount of gold increases, the bank will extend her circulation, and the pressure will subside. The principal pressures that have occurred of late years have been those of 1825, 1836, 1839, 1847, 1857 and 1866.

A season of pressure has always been preceded by one of speculation; and hence it follows that a banker who wishes to be easy in a time of pressure must act wisely in the previous season of speculation. It requires no ordinary firmness to do this. But unless a banker act wisely in the previous time of speculation, his wisdom will probably be of little avail when the pressure arrives.

Gilbart, in his "Treatise on Banking," has considerable to say about pressures, and we reproduce a few of his remarks and suggestions:—

"While, therefore, money is still abundant, the public funds high, and other bankers liberal in accommodation, he should be doubly cautious in times of pressure or of panics, and also when a severe stringency of the money market is apparent, against taking bills of a doubtful character, or making advances upon irregular securities. He should not suffer the desire of employing his funds, or the fear of offending his customers, to induce him to deviate from sound banking principles. He should also take this opportunity of calling up all dead or doubtful loans, and of getting rid of all weak customers. He should also, under any circumstances, avoid making advances for any length of time, and investments in securities that are not at all times convertible, or the price of which is likely to sustain a great fall on the occurrence of a pressure. The discount of first-rate commercial bills having a short time to run, or short loans on stock or other undesirable security, however low the interest received, seem to be the most safe and advantageous transactions.

"When the aspect of affairs seems to threaten that money will be still more in demand, and the failure of a number of merchants and traders may consequently be apprehended, it behooves him to prepare for approaching events by avoiding all discounts of bills of an inferior class, and by keeping his funds in an available state. With a view to these objects, he will review all his loan and discount accounts, call up his loans of long standing, where it can be done without injury to the interest or reputation of his bank, avoid all overdrawn accounts, and reduce the amount of discounts on the inferior class of accounts. In performing these operations, he will exercise due judgment and discretion, making proper distinction between his customers and reducing chiefly those bills which are of an unbusiness character, or which are drawn on doubtful people, or upon parties that he knows nothing about; he will also mark particularly those accounts which require large discounts, but keep no corresponding balance to the credit of their current accounts. As the pressure advances he will find that there are three demands upon his funds. First, his customers will reduce their balances, and keep less money in his hands. Money lodged at interest will be taken away, because the parties can make higher interest elsewhere, or they will be tempted by the low price of stock to invest it in government securities. Secondly, he will have a greater demand for loans and discounts, not merely from weak people whom he might not care about refusing, but from persons of known wealth, whom it is his interest and his inclination to oblige. Thirdly, he will think it prudent to guard against sudden demands by keeping a larger amount of bank notes in his possession. To meet all these demands, he will be compelled to realize on some of his securities, and he will realize those first on which he will sustain no loss.

"During a pressure a banker will have to give a great many refusals, and some discretion will be necessary in the form of giving these refusals. Let him refuse in what way he may at such a season, he will be sure to give offence. And the party refused will possibly repeat the refusal to his business acquaintances, and, from motives of ignorance or malignity, represent the refusal as having arisen from want of means, and possibly may circulate a report that the banker is about to stop payment. Hence rumors about banks are always rife in seasons of pressure, and they add to the general want of confidence which then prevails. As far as past experience goes, all panics or pressures have resulted in a subsequent abundance of money. It would be a grand thing for a banker if he could know beforehand at what precise point this change would take place. But this he cannot know, and he had better not speculate on the subject, but just follow the course of events as they occur.

"The pressure of 1847 will be briefly traced. At the meeting of Parliament in the latter end of 1847, committees were appointed by both the House of Lords and the

House of Commons, to "inquire into the causes of the distress which has for some time prevailed among the commercial classes; and how far it has been affected by the laws for regulating the issue of bank notes payable on demand."

Following is an extract from the report of the Lord's Committee as to the causes of the pressure:—

"A sudden and unexampled demand for foreign corn, produced by a failure in many descriptions of agricultural produce throughout the United Kingdom, coincided with the unprecedented extent of speculation produced by increased facilities of credit and a low rate of interest, had for some time occasioned over-trading in many branches of commerce. This was more especially felt in railroads, for which calls to a large amount were daily becoming payable, without corresponding funds to meet them, except by the withdrawal of capital from other pursuits and investments. These causes account for much of the pressure under which many of the weaker commercial firms were doomed to sink, and which was felt even by the strongest. To these causes may be added a contemporaneous rise of price in cotton; and, with respect to houses connected with the East and West India trade, a sudden and extensive fall in the price of sugar, by which the value of their most readily available assets underwent great depreciation. Some of these causes are obviously beyond the reach of legislative control. But upon those which are connected with the extension of commercial speculation, encouraged or checked by the facility or the difficulty of obtaining credit, by the advance of capital and the discount of bills, the powers and position of the Bank of England must at all times enable that corporation to exercise an important influence. The committee have consequently felt it to be their duty to inquire into the course pursued by the bank, and they have come to the conclusion that the recent panic was materially aggravated by the operation of that statute, and by the proceedings of the bank itself. This effect may be traced directly to the Act of 1844, in the legislative restriction imposed on the means of accommodation, whilst a large amount of bullion was held in the coffers of the bank, and during a time of favorable exchanges; and it may be traced to the same cause, indirectly, as a consequence of great fluctuations in the rate of discount, and of capital previously advanced at an unusually low rate of interest. This course the bank would hardly have felt itself justified in taking, had not an impression existed that, by the separation of the issue and the banking departments, one inflexible rule for regulating the bank issues has been substituted by law in place of the discretion formerly invested in the bank."

To tide over the "pressure" it was found necessary on the part of the government to call on the Bank of England again. We have been furnished a copy of the correspondence between the First Lord of the Treasury and the Chancellor of the Exchequer and the Bank of England, respecting the suspension of the Act of 1844 :—

"DOWNING STREET, Oct. 25, 1847.
"*To the Governor and Deputy-Governor of the Bank of England:—*

"GENTLEMEN :—Her Majesty's Government has seen with the deepest regret the pressure which has existed for some weeks upon the commercial interests of the country, and that this pressure has been aggravated by a want of that confidence which is necessary for carrying on the ordinary dealings of trade.

"They have been in hopes that the check given to transactions of a speculative character, the transfer of capital from other countries, the influx of bullion, and the feeling which a knowledge of these circumstances might have been expected to produce, would have removed the prevailing distrust.

"They were encouraged in this expectation by the speedy cessation of a similar state of feeling in the month of April last.

"These hopes have, however, been disappointed, and Her Majesty's Government has come to the conclusion, that the time has arrived when it ought to attempt, by some extraordinary and temporary measure, to restore confidence to the mercantile and manufacturing community.

"For this purpose, they recommend to the directors of the Bank of England, in the present emergency, to enlarge the amount of their discounts and advances upon approved security; but that, in order to retain this operation within reasonable limits, a high rate of interest should be charged.

"In present circumstances, they would suggest that the rate of interest should not be less than 8 per cent.

"If this course should lead to any infringement of the existing law, Her Majesty's Government will be prepared to propose to Parliament on its meeting, a Bill of Indemnity. They will rely upon the discretion of the directors to reduce as soon as possible the amount of their notes, if any extraordinary issue should take place, within the limits prescribed by law.

"Her Majesty's Government are of opinion that any extra profit derived from this measure should be carried to the account of the public, but the precise mode of doing so much must be left to future arrangement.

"Her Majesty's Government are not insensible of the evil of any departure from the law which has placed the currency of this country upon a sound basis; but they feel confident that, in the present circumstances, the measure which they have proposed may be safely adopted, and at the same time the main provisions of that law, and the vital principle of preserving the convertibility of the bank note, may be firmly maintained.

"We have the honor to be, gentlemen,
"Your obedient humble servants,
[Signed] "J. RUSSELL.
"CHARLES WOOD."

"To the First Lord of the Treasury and the Chancellor of the Exchequer:—
"BANK OF ENGLAND, Oct. 25, 1847.

"GENTLEMEN:—We have the honor to acknowledge your letter of this day's date, which we have submitted to the Court of Directors, and we enclose a copy of its resolutions therein:—

"*Resolved*, 1.—That this Court do accede to the recommendation contained in the letter from the First Lord of the Treasury and the Chancellor of the Exchequer, dated this day, and addressed to the governor and deputy governor of the Bank of England, which has just been read.

"2.—That the minimum rate of discount on bills not having more than ninety-five days to run be eight per cent.

"3.—That the advances be made on bills of exchange, on stock, exchequer bills, and other approved securities, in sums of not less than two thousand pounds, and for a period to be fixed by the governors, at the rate of eight per cent. per annum.

"We have the honor to be, gentlemen,
"Your most obedient servants:
"JAMES MORRIS, Governor.
"H. J. PRESCOTT, Deputy Governor."

"*To the Governor and Deputy Governor of the Bank of England:—*
"DOWNING STREET, Nov. 23, 1847.

"GENTLEMEN—Her Majesty's Government have watched, with the deepest interest, the gradual revival of confidence in the commercial classes of the country.

"They have the satisfaction of believing that the course adopted by the Bank of England, on their recommendation, has contributed to produce the result, whilst it has led to no infringement of the law.

"It appears, from the accounts which you have transmitted to us, that the reserve of the Bank of England has been for some time steadily increasing, and now amounts to £5,000,000. This increase has, in a great measure, arisen from the return of notes and coin from the country.

"The bullion exceeds £10,000,000, and the state of the exchanges promises a further influx of the precious metals.

"The knowledge of these facts by the public is calculated to inspire still further confidence.

"In these circumstances, it appears to Her Majesty's Government, that the purpose which they had in view in the letter which we addressed to you on Oct. 25, has been fully answered, and that it is unnecessary to continue that letter any longer in force.

"We have the honor to be, gentlemen,
"Your obedient, humble servants,
[Signed] "J. RUSSELL,
"CHAS. WOOD."

"*To the First Lord of the Treasury and the Chancellor of the Exchequer:*—

"BANK OF ENGLAND, Nov. 23, 1847.

"GENTLEMEN—We have the honor to acknowledge the receipt of your letter of this day's date, in which you communicate to us that in consequence of the gradual revival of confidence in the commercial classes of the country, it appears to Her Majesty's Government that the object they had in view in the letter they addressed to us on Oct. 25th has been fully answered, and that it is unnecessary to continue that letter any longer in force.

"We have the honor to be, gentlemen,
"Your obedient, humble servants,
[Signed] "JAMES MORRIS, Governor.
"H. J. PRESCOTT, Deputy Governor."

CHAPTER XXII.

A COPY OF THE CORRESPONDENCE

BETWEEN THE

CHANCELLOR OF THE EXCHEQUER

AND THE

BANK OF ENGLAND,

RELATIVE TO THE

RENEWAL OF THE CHARTER OF 1844,

Which is Treated at Length in Chapter IX, beginning on page 125.

To the Governor and Deputy Governor of the Bank of England :—

DOWNING STREET, 16th April, 1844.

GENTLEMEN—As under the provisions of the 3 and 4 W. IV. c. 98, the 1st of August is the day after which it will be competent to the House of Commons to give a notice to the Bank of England as to the termination, within a limited period, of their present exclusive privileges, Her Majesty's Government judge it advisable to endeavor to come to an understanding with the bank as to their future relation to the government, rather than to terminate the existing arrangements by recurring to the notice required by the Act of Parliament.

In submitting to you the views of the government, I would premise that the main object of the government in any new arrangement is one in the success of which the bank can be scarcely less interested than the government; namely, to place the general circulation of the country on a sounder footing, and to prevent, as much as possible, fluctuations in the currency, of the nature of those which have, at different times, occasioned hazard to the bank and embarrassment to the country.

It appears highly desirable that any new arrangement should be founded on the basis of an entire separation of the business of the issue of notes from that of banking. This measure might be effected by the establishment of a Public Department for the issue of notes independent altogether of the bank; but Her Majesty's Government is willing, in the first instance, to consider whether this can be effected by a division of the bank into two distinct and separate departments—to conduct exclusively, one the business of issue, the other that of banking. The first question for the bank to consider is, how far they are willing to undertake this duty. Should they be disposed to administer the functions of issue, it would be desirable that the following principle should be adhered to:—That a certain amount of notes should be issued on securities, and that all other notes required beyond that amount should be issued only in exchange for bullion—that the securities should be, to a certain extent, of such a nature as to admit of ready convertibility, and should not be increased beyond the amount originally fixed, except under circumstances to be stated by the bank to the government; and after the consent of certain members of the government, namely, the First Lord of the Treasury, the Chancellor of the Exchequer, and the Master of the Mint, shall have been signified.

It is proposed from henceforth to prohibit the establishment of any new bank of issue; to restrict the issue of their own notes to those banks at present exercising that privilege, and to limit the issue of such banks to the amount of notes issued by them on an average of a given preceding period, and in the event of their failure or liquidation, to prohibit under any circumstances, the resumption of their own circulation. The void created by the withdrawal of any existing private or joint-stock bank circulation, either voluntarily or under the circumstances adverted to, should be supplied, if necessary, by the substitution of notes of the Bank of England; and, in such a case, the bank acting in concert with the government, as provided for in a preceding paragraph, might be authorized to make a proportionate increase in the amount of those securities which constitute the foundation of the issue of paper; the whole net profit derived from this additional issue would be carried to the account of the government, and would be in addition to the annual payment which the bank may agree to make.

It is intended that a weekly publication should take place, showing the state of both the issue and banking departments of the bank, and it will be required that each private and joint-stock bank issuing its own notes, should make once a week a publication of the amount of their notes in circulation.

Under such an arrangement, it is obvious that the bank will not merely retain its existing privileges of having no bank of more than six partners issuing notes within sixty-five miles of London, but will be secured against the competition within that district, of any new banks of issue, even with less than six partners, which might otherwise be established; and although, as the profit of any increased issue will be placed henceforth to the account of the government, the bank will not derive direct pecuniary advantage, yet the extension of business and of confidence in the bank (which must result from the extension of its notes consequent upon this further exclusion) must be to the bank a source of no inconsiderable benefit.

I must add, that it is not proposed to continue the prohibition which is now in force as to the drawing, accepting, or paying bills, within the sixty-five mile circle around London.

Should an arrangement on these principles meet the views of the bank, the points remaining for consideration will be, the period for which the bank charter shall be renewed, and the amount of the payment which ought to be made by the bank to the public during the period of its continuance.

Her Majesty's Government considers it advisable that the charter should be granted for ten years, from the 1st of August, 1845, and should, at the expiration of that period, be terminable at any time upon a notice of twelve months, but, until such notice be given, should continue in force. The amount of payment to be made to the public by the bank will depend upon a joint consideration of the benefits secured by this arrangement to the banking department of the bank, and of the proportion of the profits of the issue or circulation department, which the public is entitled to claim. As bankers, the bank will retain the management of the public debt, and the advantage of the government deposits and the balances of the several public accounts at the bank. It must, however, be distinctly understood, that the government retains an entire discretion as to the amount of such deposits to be left in the hands of the bank, and as to a participation in the profits of such deposits, if they should, from any circumstances, be materially increased.

With respect to the profits of the circulation department, supposing the fixed amount of securities to be £14,000,000, the profit would, obviously, be the difference between the interest received on those securities and the expenditure required for the manufacture and issue of the notes, the keeping of the accounts connected with them, and the receipt and custody of the bullion, which might, from time to time, come into the hands of that department.

Assuming three per cent. as the rate of interest, the gross profit of the circulation department would be £420,000.

It was stated by the bank, in a paper presented to the committee on the bank charter in 1832, that the expense of the circulation was at that time £106,000. It would be desirable that the items constituting this aggregate sum should be separately considered, with a view of ascertaining whether, without diminishing the advantages now afforded to the public, a reduction might not be effected in the amount. I will, however, assume it, for my present purpose, as amounting to £100,000.

A sum of £320,000 would then remain as the profit of the circulation department, from which would have to be further deducted the amount of stamp duty paid on the notes of the Bank of England, being about £60,000, and the sum, whatever it may be, which the bank now allows to those banks of issue which have substituted Bank of England notes for their own paper, and which I assume, for the purpose of discussion, as about £20,000. The net profits, therefore, in which the public would have a right to share, would be a sum of £240,000, or, if it were thought more advisable to remove the stamp duty on the notes of the bank, £300,000. In fixing the proportion of this amount which ought to be paid to the public, I do not on the one hand put out of view the fair claim of the bank to compensation, as managers on behalf of the public of the circulation of the country; but, on the other hand, the bank will not fail to bear in mind that, by the advance of their capital of £11,000,000 to the public at 3 per cent., they have hitherto virtually paid to the public a sum little short of one per cent. on that amount; and that now, owing to the present circumstances of the country, that advance is no longer any sacrifice on the part of the bank, nor any compensation to the public for the benefit derived to the bank from its connection with the government. It may, therefore, justly become a question, whether that debt of the public to the bank should be continued at its present amount, or at its present rate of interest.

It appears to me, therefore, that in claiming for the public an annual payment exceeding that now made by the bank, while I reserve also to the public the net profit which may result from any addition hereafter to be made to the amount of fixed securities, I am not claiming more than the bank will deem a just compensation for the advantages secured to them.

It appears to me that the real interests of the bank, taking a comprehensive view of those interests, will be materially promoted by the proposed arrangement. It proposes to leave to them the management of the circulation; it gives a new and decisive proof of the public confidence reposed in them, while the measure itself is calculated, by increasing the control of the bank over the paper currency of the country, to secure them from much expense and danger to which they have hitherto been exposed.

I have the honor to be,
gentlemen,
Your very faithful and obedient servant,
[Signed]   HENRY GOULBURN.

To the Right Honorable, the Chancellor of the Exchequer, M. P.

BANK OF ENGLAND, April 30, 1884.

SIR:— We have the honor to acknowledge the receipt of your letter of the 26th instant, which we have submitted to the consideration of the Committee of Treasury and of the Court of Directors, and we are desired to assure you that they, in common with ourselves, are duly impressed with the importance of an early settlement of the question affecting the circulation of the country, and are satisfied that the bank, relinquishing its claim to the notice prescribed by law, will give its most favorable consideration to any proposal from Her Majesty's Ministers having for its object to place the circulation of the country on a sounder footing.

To the "Entire separation of the business of Issue of Notes from that of Banking," we are not disposed to offer any objection, and are of opinion that a division of the bank into two distinct and separate departments for that object, can be affected without difficulty; neither do we differ respecting the principles of the intended measures detailed in your letter.

It is now proposed to take from the bank all the future advantages that may arise from the substitution of its notes for the present issues of joint-stock and private banks. We are prepared to admit the favorable impression which the public opinion will receive from the fact of the bank having no pecuniary interest in the more general adoption of its notes. It must, however, be recollected that under the arrangement of 1833, by which it was agreed to allow to the public £120,000 per annum, very considerable advantages were held out to the bank from the extension of its circulation; these were never realized, in consequence of the declared inability of the government to carry into effect the measures on which that speculation was founded.

As the government considers that "A weekly publication should take place of the state both of the issue and banking departments of the bank, and that each joint stock and private bank, issuing its own paper, should make, once a week, a publication of the amount of its notes in circulation," the court would raise no objection to that arrangement; but we would suggest, for the consideration of the government, if the publication of the banking accounts can be regarded as essential?

By the removal of "The prohibition now in force, as to the drawing, accepting, or paying bills within the sixty-five mile circle around London," the bank may incur some loss in its banking department; but more serious inconvenience will result, if the power to accept should be exercised for the purpose of circulation, and thus interfere with the great object of the projected measures; a question deserving the most serious consideration.

On the subject of the proposed grant of the bank charter for ten years from the 1st August, 1845, subject at the end of that period to terminate upon a notice of twelve months, but until such notice be given to continue in force; we would suggest as a preferable plan, that if notice shall not be given by the government at the end of ten years, the charter should continue until after the expiration of an additional period of ten years. It seems to us that sufficient power of control would thus be retained by the government, and that the inconvenience arising from repeated, if not annual, discussions on the subject, would thus be avoided.

The possession of the £11,000,000 advanced by the bank has ever been considered as affording additional security to the public, and contributing to that entire confidence at all times placed in the solidity of the bank; and, although, at an interest of 3 per cent., the loan may not at this moment impose any pecuniary sacrifice on the bank, we see no benefit likely to arise to the public from its repayment. We, therefore, think it for the public good that it should still be retained; and we would, at the same time, remark that any reduction in the interest on this loan will necessarily diminish to a corresponding extent, the profit in the issue department of the bank.

Referring to the estimate of the profit to be derived from the department of issue, we must remark that we calculate its actual expense at £113,000 per annum; a large outlay being incurred for the sole accommodation of the public by bank notes, not being reissued in London; by the complete registration of the issue and cancelment of each note; by the preservation of the cancelled notes for ten years for the purpose of legal reference, so that each note can, in case of need, be traced, and frauds thus be detected; and finally, by the ready supply of notes for bullion or coin, besides various other arrangements adopted solely for the public convenience. A reissue of notes was commenced, as a measure of economy, in the year 1838, but so much inconvenience was experienced by the bankers and the public, that it was abandoned; and the bank now issues about 20,000 notes, averaging in amount from six to seven hundred thousand pounds, cancelling also the same number and value, daily.

The allowance at present made to those joint-stock and private banks under engagement to issue only Bank of England paper, will, at one per cent., amount to twenty-four thousand pounds, as appears by the Parliamentary return; and we submit the following as the correct calculation, viz.:—

£14,000,000 at 3 per cent.		£420,000
Deduct the expense	£113,000	
Present allowance to the banks and banking companies	24,000	137,000
		£283,000

before any payment is made to the government.

In reference to the position of the bank, as having the management of the public debt and the benefit of the government deposits, we wish to state that the advantage from the former is diminished by the great risk of forgery, and from the latter by the alteration of the exchequer accounts in 1834, which considerably reduced the amount of the public balances; but, in reply to the proposed understanding that the government will retain an entire discretion as to the amount of such deposits, as to a participation in the profits arising from them, if they should, from any circumstances, be materially increased, we beg to say that we should not object to this, provided it is conceded by the government that an allowance will be made to the bank if the balances are reduced below their present amount.

The benefits to the bank will also be further reduced by the expenses which will be incurred in the collection of the ordinary revenue; and, in reference to these, it should be stated that, in the year 1843, the clerks of the bank travelled on the revenue account, 75,090 miles, with the risk attending the custody and transit of £9,047,000, the money being brought immediately to the credit of the government, saving to the public a considerable amount of interest and risk. Taking these circumstances into consideration, and bearing in mind that, under the proposed arrangement, the bank will derive no advantage from the extension of its circulation, with all the responsibility, an abatement from the £120,000 hitherto allowed to the public may reasonably be expected; for if the bank continue this payment to the government, together with a liability to the estimated amount of the stamp duty on the notes issued on the fourteen millions of securities, viz., £49,000, making a total of £169,000, and incur, besides, the whole responsibility of the extended circulation without profit, the court is of opinion that it will be called upon to make a larger sacrifice than in reason and justice can be required.

We have the honor to be,
Sir,
Your very faithful and obedient servants,
[Signed]   WILLIAM COTTON, Governor.
J. B. HEATH, Deputy Governor.

To the Governor and Deputy Governor of the Bank of England :—
DOWNING STREET, May 2, 1844.

GENTLEMEN—I have the honor to acknowledge the receipt of your letter of the 30th ultimo.

It is satisfactory to Her Majesty's Government to learn that there is on the part of the Bank of England a general concurrence in the principle of the proposal conveyed in my letter of the 27th ultimo, and a readiness to coöperate in giving effect to them.

They observe with pleasure that, notwithstanding the doubts which you suggested as to its utility, you offer no objection to a weekly publication of the state of the banking as well as of the issue department.

That measure was recommended to you on behalf of the government, under the conviction that such a publication would be advantageous to the public, and would carry with it the strongest evidence of the stability and credit of the institution over which your preside, and upon the same grounds it still appears to the government to be of essential importance.

I agree with you that if the removal of the existing prohibition against accepting bills within the sixty-five mile circle around London should lead to the introduction of a new paper circulation, it might materially intercfere with the object of the proposed arrangement. An attempt might undoubtedly be made now to guard against such an evil consequence, by imposing generally, and in the case of all banking establishments, a limit upon the sum for which the bills to be accepted might be drawn, or by extending the dates at which they might become payable. But, while such a measure might fail in proving an effective check upon future evasions, it is calculated to raise impediments in the way of legitimate banking business. It appears, therefore, more advisable to trust for a remedy for so serious an evil to the power of the government—a power which will not fail to be exercised if the abuse should arise—of applying by new legislative enactment an adequate corrective.

Her Majesty's Government has well weighed the reasons which you have urged for preferring a renewal of the charter upon the terms granted in 1833, namely, for twenty years, with the power of terminating it at a notice given at the expiration of ten.

In making the proposal contained in my letter of the

27th ultimo, the government was mainly influenced by the consideration, to which you appear also to attach much weight, that it was not advisable unnecessarily to agitate questions affecting the banking interests and the currency of the country.

We confidently hope that the arrangements now to be made will be found at the end of ten years to have satisfied public expectation, and in that case there would probably be a disposition, encouraged by the knowledge that the subject was at any time open to discussion, to forbear from proposing a change in the existing system. But on the other hand, if the opportunity of revision afforded at the end of ten years were not again to occur till the expiration of a similiar period, the necessity of reviewing what was otherwise to be for so long a time irrevocable, could scarcely be denied.

On those grounds Her Majesty's Government considers that it would be more for the public interests that the charter should be continued as proposed in my former letter.

The reasons offered by you for the retention by the public of the £11,000,000 advanced by the bank, are entitled to considerable weight; and in the event of the acquiescence of the bank in the terms proposed, Her Majesty's Government is prepared to consent to that debt remaining during the further continuance of the charter on its present footing.

With respect to the public balances in the hands of the bank, I deem it unnecessary to make any observation. The government must necessarily retain an unfettered discretion as to the amount which it may be proper to keep in the bank, and in the event of any extraordinary accumulation beyond the usual amount, it would be hereafter, as it has been heretofore, competent to them to make any arrangement with the bank which might appear to them conducive to the public interests.

With reference to the expense of the department of issue, I readily admit the importance of not discontinuing any one of the facilities which the bank has hitherto afforded to the public, although necessarily attended with an increase of charge. Nor, after a due consideration of the detail of the expenditure of £113,000, which you have assigned to the issue department, am I prepared to state that it is excessive.

But after making the deductions which you have specified, the profit of the issue department still amounts to £983,000.

Under these circumstances, I cannot feel myself authorized to hold out to the bank any expectation of an abatement from the sum of £120,000, which they now allow to the public; nor can I admit the payment of £49,000 to be an adequate compensation for the sum which would accrue to the public from leaving the Bank of England notes still subject to stamp duty. The sum latterly received on this account has been, as I previously stated, £60,000. I should certainly have preferred the continued payment by the bank of duty on the amount of notes in circulation. By the arrangement, however, which I have proposed, the public will henceforth be entitled to receive the whole net profit of any issue of notes founded on any addition to the fixed amount of securities.

The stamp duty on such notes would necessarily be a

deduction from the profit for which the bank have to account; and I anticipate considerable difficulty, in the case of such additional issue, of ascertaining the precise proportion of such issue which might be in circulation, and on which alone the duty would attach. I am, therefore, prepared, on behalf of the government, to accept, as compensation for the stamp duty a sum of £60,000.

If, therefore, the Bank of England is prepared to make a fixed annual payment to the public, amounting in the whole to £180,000, subject to the several conditions which I have in this and in my former letter submitted to you, Her Majesty's Government will be prepared to recommend to Parliament the continuance of the charter for the period for which I have specified.

I have the honor to be,
gentlemen,
Your most obedient servant,
[Signed] HENRY GOULBURN.

To the Right Honorable, the Chancellor of the Exchequer:—

BANK OF ENGLAND, May 3, 1844,

SIR:—We have the honor to acknowedge your letter of the 2d inst., which we have submitted to the consideraation of the Court of Directors; and although they are still of the opinion that some abatement from the £120,000 allowed to the public might reasonably have been expected, they have resolved, in order that no obstacle may be presented by them to the measures which are considered desirable by Her Majesty's Ministers to place the currency on a sounder footing, to recommend to the Court of Proprietors to accede to the proposals of the government.

We have the honor to be,
Sir,
Your very faithful and obedient servants,
[Signed] WILLIAM COTTON, Governor.
J. B. HEATH, Deputy Governor.

CHAPTER XXIII.

AMERICAN AND ENGLISH BANKERS ASSOCIATIONS.

Constitution of the American Bankers' Association—Who are Eligible to Membership—Its Objects—How Conducted—The English Institute of Bankers—Its Constitution—Facilities Afforded to Members—Detailed Account of the Manner of Conducting Business.

DECLARATION.

IN order to promote the general welfare and usefulness of banks and banking institutions, and to secure uniformity of action, together with the practical benefits to be derived from personal acquaintance and from the discussion of subjects of importance to the banking and commercial interests of the country; and especially in order to secure the proper consideration of questions regarding the financial and commercial usages, customs and laws which affect the banking interests of the entire country, and for protection against loss by crime, we have to submit the following Constitution and By-Laws for "The American Bankers Association:"

CONSTITUTION.

Article I.

Section 1. This Association shall be called "THE AMERICAN BANKERS ASSOCIATION."

Article II.

Sec. 1. Any National or State Bank, Trust Company, Savings Bank or Banking Firm may become a member of this Association upon the payment of such annual dues as shall be provided by the by-laws, and may send one delegate to the annual meetings of the Association; and any member may be expelled from the Association upon a vote of two-thirds of those present at any regular meeting.

Sec. 2. Delegates shall be an officer or director, or trustee of the institutions they represent, or a member of a banking firm, or an individual doing business as a bank.

Sec. 3. Delegates shall vote in person; no voting by proxy shall be allowed.

Sec. 4. All votes shall be *viva voce*, unless otherwise ordered; any delegate may demand a division of the house.

Article III.

Sec. 1. The administration of the affairs of this Association shall be vested in the President and Vice-President of this Association, and one Vice-President for each State and Territory which may be represented in this Association, and in an Executive Council, composed of twenty-one members of this Association, who shall be elected at the annual meetings, and who shall serve until their successors are chosen or appointed, but none of whom shall hereafter be eligible for election to the same office for more than three consecutive years.

Sec. 2. The vice-presidents shall have the supervision of the business of the Association in the States and Territories where they reside, and may call meetings when they may deem the same necessary; and in case of absence or disability of the president or first vice-president of the Association to preside, they may designate one of their number to act as president *pro tem.;* and said president *pro tem.* shall, in case of death or other disability of the president, be invested with all the power of president until a successor shall be duly elected or appointed.

Sec. 3. The executive council of twenty-one shall take charge of the general business of the Association, receive communications, arrange for holding meetings, procure and arrange subjects for discussion in the order in which they may come before the convention, provide for speakers, and carry out the resolutions passed. They shall also act as a financial committee for raising and disbursing moneys. The attendance of five members of the executive council shall constitute a quorum for the transaction of business.

Sec. 4. The executive council of twenty-one may appoint and discharge the secretary and treasurer, or other employees of the Association, at their discretion.

Sec. 5. Special meetings of the executive council may be called by request of three of its own members, giving two weeks' notice to the secretary desiring him to call such special meeting. The council shall have power to fill vacancies that may occur in their own body.

Sec. 6. The executive council shall provide — 1st, for keeping the records of the proceedings of their own meetings, as well as that of the Association's annual or special meetings; 2d, they shall submit to each annual meeting a report, covering their own official acts as well as a statement of any new or unfinished business requiring attention ; 3d, they shall make full statements of the financial condition of the Association; and 4th, submit an estimate of the amount required to carry on the affairs of the Association according to their judgmemt of the business to be done, and recommend means for raising money to carry out such plans as may be resolved upon by the Association.

Sec. 7. The secretary shall make and have charge of the records of the Association, as well as those of the council, and of the correspondence of the executive council and standing protective committee, and shall promptly send to each member of the Association a synopsis of reports received by him of attempted or accomplished crime against any member of the Association. Such records shall be the property of this Association, and be held subject at all times to the order of the executive council.

Sec. 8. The treasurer shall receive and account for all moneys belonging to the Association, and collect dues; but shall pay out moneys only upon vouchers countersigned and approved by the president of the Association, or by the secretary appointed by the executive council.

ARTICLE IV.

Sec. 1. The executive council shall appoint a *Standing Protective Committee* of three persons, whose names shall not be made public. The said committee shall control all action looking to the detection, prosecution and punishment of persons attempting to cause or causing loss, by crime, to any member of the Association.

Sec. 2. The said committee, when called upon for aid, by any member of the Association, through the secretary, shall forthwith take such steps as it shall deem proper to arrest and prosecute the party charged with crime.

Sec. 3. The said committee is prohibited from compromising or compounding with parties charged with crime, or with their agents or attorneys.

Sec. 4. All detective and legal expenses and costs shall be paid by the Association out of any moneys in the treasury not otherwise appropriated; subject, however, to the approval of a quorum of the executive council.

Sec. 5. All members of the Association, when called upon by the secretary in behaf of the protective committee for information or aid, shall promptly respond by giving all assistance in their power; and all members shall, at all times, notify the secretary, who shall promptly notify the committee, of any attempted or accomplished crime reported to him as likely to affect other members of the Association.

ARTICLE V.

Sec. 1. Annual meetings of the Association shall be held at such times and places as shall be determined by the executive council. Special meetings may be called by the council if, in their opinion, circumstances require them, giving *two weeks*' notice of the time and place of meeting, together with the subject matter of business to come before such special meeting. The executive council shall meet to arrange the order of business on the day preceding meeting of Association.

Article VI.

Sec. 1. The expenses of the executive council of the Association, in carrying out the business to be done by them, shall be provided for by the annual dues of the members of the Association; provided, however, that the executive council shall have no authority to incur or contract on behalf of this Association any liability whatever beyond the annual dues hereby authorized, and only that for the purposes hereby designated.

Article VII.

Sec. 1. Resolutions or subjects for discussion (except those referring to points of order or matters of courtesy) must be submitted to the executive council in writing at least *thirty days* before any general meeting of the Association; but any person desiring to submit any resolution or business in open convention can do so upon a two-thirds vote of the delegates present, referring the resolution to the executive council or committee on resolutions to report upon immediately.

Article VIII.

Any one failing to pay within three months the annual dues for carrying on the business of the Association, shall be considered as having withdrawn from membership, but may be reinstated upon application to the treasurer, and paying all dues in arrears, with consent of the president.

Article IX.

This constitution may be altered or amended at any annual meeting by a vote of two-thirds of the members present, notice of the proposed amendment having been first submitted to the secretary at least thirty days before the annual meeting, to be placed by him before the executive council, that they may arrange for bringing it before the convention under the regular order of business.

BY-LAWS

OF THE AMERICAN BANKERS ASSOCIATION.

The annual dues to the Association shall be considered due at the beginning of the year, which year shall commence with the regular annual meeting, it being understood that absent members from such annual meeting shall not forfeit their membership nor the right to become members, provided they comply with the constitution and by-laws, and remit the amount of the dues to the treasurer within three months after such annual meeting.

The annual dues of all banks and trust companies having less than $100,000 capital, and of all private bankers, regardless of the amount of capital, shall be $5, and of all banks and trust companies having a capital of $100,000 and upwards, $10.

CONSTITUTION

OF THE

INSTITUTE OF BANKERS.

1. The name of the Institue is "The Institute of Bankers." (Was founded in London in 1879.)

2. The Institute is an association of gentlemen connected with the various branches of banking. Its primary object is to facilitate the consideration and discussion of matters of interest to the profession, and, where advisable, to take measures to further the decisions arrived at ; and its secondary object is to afford opportunities for the acquisition of a knowledge of the theory of banking.

3. The Institute shall afford facilities for the reading, discussion, and publication of approved papers by members and others; shall, when desirable, recognize and arrange for the delivery of lectures on banking, mercantile law, political economy, and other kindred subjects; shall issue certificates to those who may pass examinations approved of from time to time by the council of the Institute; and shall found a library, consisting of works on banking, commerce, finance, and political economy.

4. If the council shall at any time, or from time to time, think it desirable to acquire for the purposes of the Institute the whole or part of any building or buildings, they shall have power to purchase or lease the same upon

such terms as they shall think fit, and they shall also have power from time to time to sell or surrender any premises which, in their judgment, are no longer required for such objects.

5. The members of the Institute are Fellows, Associates, and Ordinary Members:—

Fellows shall be elected by the council. Each applicant for admission as a fellow shall be nominated by two or more fellows, who shall certify in writing that the candidate is a fit person to be elected a Fellow of the Institute of Bankers.

The council shall have power to elect as honorary fellows men of distinction in the practice or literature of banking, mercantile law, political economy, or other kindred subjects.

Associates shall in future be elected by the council from those who have been not less than ten years in the service of any bank; or from those who have passed the examination instituted or recognized by the council, or from those who, being on the staff of a bank, are graduates of any university. Each applicant for admission as an associate shall in every case be proposed by two fellows of the Institute, who shall certify in writing that the candidate is a fit person to be elected an Associate of the Institute of Bankers.

Ordinary Members—clerks on the staff of any banking establishment, and who shall be approved by the council.

6. Associate and ordinary members, as well as fellows, shall have the right to be present at the various meetings of the Institute; but in any case when any election

is to be made, or the opinion or decision of the Institute is to be taken on any subject or question by vote, at any meeting, ordinary or special, the fellows and associates of the Institute shall, except where otherwise specially provided by the constitution, alone be entitled to vote.

7. The control of the Institute shall be vested in the president, vice-presidents, treasurer, and council for the time being.

8. The president, vice-presidents, and treasurer shall *ex-officio* be members of the council. They shall be elected each year, at the annual general meeting, from among the fellows of the Institute. Each shall be eligible for re-election, and shall hold office until his successor is appointed.

The council shall be not more than twenty-four in number, exclusive of the president, vice-presidents, and treasurer. At each annual general meeting six members of the council shall retire from office. The order of retirement shall be determined by the council. Each shall be eligible for re-election. At each annual general meeting, a sufficient number of members of council shall be elected from among the fellows to supply the places of those retiring.

The notice convening the annual general meeting shall state the names of those recommended by the council for election as president, vice-presidents, treasurer, and as members of council to supply the places of those retiring.

9. On any extraordinary vacancy of the office of the president, or any officer other than trustee of the Institute, or in the council, a meeting of the council shall be

summoned with as little delay as possible, and shall choose a new president or other officer of the Institute, or member of the council, as the case may be, to hold office until the next annual general meeting.

10. AUDITORS—At the annual general meeting in each year, two fellows of the Institute, not being members of the council, shall be elected to act as auditors for the ensuing year.

The auditors shall hold office until the next annual general meeting, and shall be eligible for re-election.

11. TRUSTEES—The property of the Institute shall be vested in three trustees, and a resolution of the council shall, in all cases, be a sufficient authority and protection to the trustees for and in respect of any conveyance, transfer, payment, or other act thereby directed. Each trustee, whether already appointed or to be appointed, shall hold such office until his death, resignation or removal.

Any trustee may retire from office on giving a written notice, addressed to the council, of his desire so to do. Any trustee may be removed, at a special general meeting, if it shall be determined at the meeting that sufficient cause exists for such removal, and any vacancy in the office of trustee may be supplied from among the fellows at the same or any other special general meeting.

12. The council shall appoint two or more of their number to be honorary secretaries, and engage such paid officers as they from time to time deem necessary.

13. The council shall meet once a month, or oftener, as may be requisite. Five members to be a quorum.

14. The council may, from time to time, issue a jour-

nal or such other publication as they may think desirable, and for this purpose appoint one of their members to be honorary editor, and engage such paid assistance, and apply in paying the expenses of the journal such part of the funds of the Institute as in their judgment may be necessary.

15. The subscriptions to the Institute shall be two guineas for fellows, one guinea for associates, and ten shillings and sixpence for ordinary members, payable annually, in advance, on the 1st of January in each year, which may be compounded for by payment, at any one time, of twenty guineas for fellows and ten guineas for associates. One year's subscription shall be payable on admission, unless the date of admission be later than the 30th of June, when only a half year's subscription shall be so payable.

16. Any fellow, associate, or ordinary member who shall not have paid his subscription before the 1st of March in any year, may be declared a defaulter by the council, whereupon he shall cease to be a member of the Institute.

17. Any fellow, associate, or ordinary member may resign, on giving notice of his intention, in writing, to the council; but no one can withdraw his name from the books of the Institute unless his subscription shall have been paid for the year in which the notice of his resignation is received.

18. A majority of not less than three-fourths of the council present at a meeting, special notice having been given for that purpose, may remove from the books of the Institute the name of any fellow, associate, or ordinary

member, who, in their judgment, shall have been guilty of any act derogatory to his character, reputation, and calculated to bring discredit on the Institute, and he shall thereupon cease to be a member of the Institute.

19. The ordinary general meeting of the Institute shall be monthly or oftener during the session, which shall be from October to May, both inclusive, on such days and at such hours as the council shall declare. The council may, when it appears to be necessary, and shall, on the written requisition of not less than fifty members of the Institute, of whom not less than fifteen shall be fellows, call a special general meeting of the Institute.

20. A general meeting of fellows, associates, and ordinary members shall be held once in every year, at such time as the council may determine, to receive the report of the council and the treasurer's accounts, to elect the officers of the Institute, and to decide questions concerning its rules and management.

21. All elections, whether by the council, or otherwise, shall be by ballot, and, except where the constitution shall otherwise provide, all elections and all questions shall be determined by a majority of votes.

22. A majority of the fellows, associates, and members present at a special general meeting shall have power to make, from time to time, any alterations in the constitution, not inconsistent with its main object, but no alteration shall be made without notice of the proposed alteration having been given in the notice convening the meeting, nor until the minutes of such meeting have been confirmed at a subsequent general meeting, ordinary or special, at which subsequent meeting ordinary members,

as well as fellows and associates, shall have the right to vote.

23. All notices of general meetings shall be either delivered at, or sent by post to, the last known place of business of each member of the Institute ten days at least before the day of the meeting. Every notice of a special general meeting shall specify the object with which such meeting is convened.

24. The council may, from time to time, make such by-laws, not inconsistent with this constitution, as in their judgment may be necessary or desirable in the interests of the Institute.

25. All persons, admitted either as fellows, associates, or ordinary members, shall, upon their admissions, sign a declaration (in the form annexed) to observe the rules, regulations, and by-laws of the Institute for the time being in force.

DECLARATION OF MEMBERSHIP.

I do hereby declare that I will endeavor to further the good of the Institute of Bankers and the ends for which the same has been founded, and that I will keep and fulfill the rules and orders of the Institute, provided that whensoever I shall make known in writing under my hand, to the Council for the time being, that I desire to withdraw from the Institute, I shall be free thenceforward from this obligation.

0

www.ingramcontent.com/pod-product-compliance
Lightning Source LLC
Chambersburg PA
CBHW022027240426
4366 7CB000042B/1218